AMAZING STORIES

LUCKY LUCIANO

AMAZING STORIES

LUCKY LUCIANO

The Father of Organized Crime

GANGSTER

by Cat Klerks

PUBLISHED BY ALTITUDE PUBLISHING LTD.
1500 Railway Avenue, Canmore, Alberta T1W 1P6
www.altitudepublishing.com
1-800-957-6888

First published 2005

Publisher	Stephen Hutchings
Associate Publisher	Kara Turner
Series Editor	Jill Foran
Editor	Marial Shea
Digital Photo Colouring	Bryan Pezzi

We acknowledge the financial support of the Government of Canada through the Book Publishing Industry Development Program (BPIDP) for our publishing activities.

Altitude GreenTree Program
Altitude Publishing will plant twice as many trees as were used in the manufacturing of this product.

Cataloguing in Publication Data

Klerks, Cat
Lucky Luciano / Cat Klerks.

(Amazing stories)
Includes bibliographical references.
ISBN 1-55265-102-9

1. Luciano, Lucky, 1897-1962. 2. Criminals--New York (State)--New York--Biography. 3. Organized crime--New York (State)--New York. I. Title. II. Series: Amazing stories (Canmore, Alta.)

HV6248.L92K54 2005 364.1'092 C2005-901370-2

Printed and bound in Canada by Friesens
2 4 6 8 9 7 5 3 1

The history of organized crime in New York City has long been glamorized through books, magazines, film, and television. Inevitably, anyone researching this history will be presented with many different "true accounts" of underworld events. In regards to each title in the Amazing Stories series, Altitude Publishing has left it up to the author to choose which version of events he or she wishes to convey.

For my sisters

Contents

Prologue

Back home, it was winter. Snowstorms raged, fires crackled on the hearth, and children dreamed of Christmas delights. Here, in this island paradise, the windows were thrown open wide, allowing cooling night breezes to blow in off the sea.

The hotel guests leaned back in their plush armchairs, signaling the white-jacketed waiters for rum punch and other exotic, fruit-filled drinks. They dabbed at their foreheads with sweat-dampened handkerchiefs, loosened their silk ties, shrugged off their tailored jackets. Ash fell from the tips of their Cuban cigars and scorched the expensive rugs underfoot, but the men were oblivious to this destruction. Though they had the look of prosperous businessmen, something cold and disturbing lay behind their eyes.

It had been a decade and a half since these men had last gathered together. From time to time, someone would catch sight of an old comrade and leap to his feet with a joyful cry of recognition. As glasses clinked and chandeliers sparkled overhead, men embraced each other in the Italian tradition, with a smacking kiss to each cheek.

Then, at the urging of the crowd, the skinny, blue-eyed guest of honor rose from his seat. The music swelled. With microphone in hand, he dazzled his audience with an impromptu medley of his greatest hits. The room erupted with cheers, whistles, and applause. The kid from Jersey was one of their own, after all.

But there was another man in the spotlight that night, a figure as threatening as he was charming. With his scarred, pitted features and sinister, drooping eye, this man would never get the bobbysoxers screaming the way Frank did. In his own way, though, he was just as influential. And far, far more dangerous ...

Chapter 1
The Life and Death of Salvatore Lucania

The year is 1916, and a young Italian immigrant named Salvatore Lucania is at a crossroads. With a string of petty convictions behind him, the future looks bleak for the high school dropout. But all is not yet lost. At the urging of his tearful mother and quick-fisted father, he has made an effort to go "straight" and has landed a job with the Goodman Hat Company, delivering their creations to some of the tonier addresses in New York City.

But the plan to go legit backfires. Salvatore — or Charlie, as he prefers to be called — soon realizes that the bulky cardboard hatboxes he tucks under his arm could easily accommodate another, more profitable cargo. As an errand boy, he is able to roam the city streets without attracting undue attention — the perfect cover for an illegal operation. "If I can deliver hats," he thinks," then I can deliver other things."

The catch, though, is there is always the chance Charlie will be caught by the police. If they apprehend him, he risks losing his job, his parents' respect, even his freedom. But Charlie has been a gambler since he first tossed the dice in a kids' back-alley craps game. The odds, he thinks, are in his favor, and the pay-off a big one. Soon, Charlie is supplementing his income as a drug mule, delivering shipments of heroin throughout the city.

The scheme is over almost before it has begun. The men in blue have been keeping an eye on his supplier, and Charlie is nabbed carrying a shipment of the deadly white powder. He loudly protests his innocence, but the cops aren't buying it. Charlie has been known to them since he was barely 10 years old. Back then, the offence was taking a "five-finger discount" — shoplifting. The wide-eyed youngster was let off with a slap on the wrist and a promise of good behavior. But the insolent, thuggish youth of 19 is not so fortunate. He is hauled off to court and, as his mother, Rosalia, weeps and wails, the judge sentences him to the Hampton Farms Penitentiary, where he is given the chance to repent, or better yet, to reform.

After serving half of his year-long sentence, Charlie emerges from his cell a changed man. Six months spent scrubbing stone floors and avoiding senseless beatings from the guards have taught him several valuable lessons, though not the kind his parents, or the courts, were intending: never rat out your friends and associates and never, ever, get caught red-handed.

The Lucanias' worst fears are soon realized, despite their hopes for Charlie's rehabilitation. When Antonio Lucania finds an expensive gold belt buckle hidden in the back of a chest of drawers, he is forced to confront the fact that his beloved boy is a thief and a liar. Screaming obscenities and throwing punches, he orders the boy to leave the family home and never return, as the four other children watch silently on the sidelines. This is all the prompting the young man needs. With a casual "So long, Mom, I'm leaving," Charlie is out of the house and on the streets.

In reality, it was even worse than the Lucanias could have imagined. Charlie, their charming, good-natured son, was actually a rising member of New York's Five Points Gang, an outfit devoted to violence and mayhem. His closest friends were muggers, thieves, gamblers, and worse. Among his fellow gang members was an old school friend, one Alphonse Capone, soon to become known as Scarface Al, the most famous mobster of all time. The two were so close that Al jokingly called the newly sprung jailbird "Cousin Charlie," predicting great things for his partner in crime. But at this point, both Al and Charlie were still little fish in a big pond. Charlie could barely even afford the three dollars he needed to rent a squalid room in a decaying tenement building. He was sometimes forced to rely on the homemade pasta sauce his mother occasionally brought over just to keep him going.

Overseas, World War I raged. In an effort to put a quick end to the fighting, the United States government had just instituted the draft. Many of the boys he went to school with ended up in uniform, but Charlie, who suffered from not one but two sexually transmitted diseases, was exempted from army service, much to his relief. Here on home soil, Lucania, Capone, and untold others were infantrymen in an army of criminals, obediently selling drugs, robbing banks, even committing murder when their superiors ordered them to do so, while making only a fraction of the profits.

But it wasn't Scarface Al who was Charlie's strongest ally. That position was filled by a skinny, soft-spoken kid five years his junior, Maier Suchowljansky, more commonly known as Meyer Lansky. The two first met when they were schoolboys. Even at that tender age, Charlie had a racket going on. He would sidle up to younger, smaller children and make them an offer they couldn't refuse. If they were smart, he said, they would voluntarily hand over all their pocket money to him. If they declined, he threatened to pound them into the pavement. Most took one look at his menacing figure and quickly handed over their change. Meyer, the puny Jewish kid, struck Charlie as an easy mark. He approached his young prey, raised his fists, and made his usual offer. To his amazement, Meyer refused to pay, and put up his dukes as well. The two boys fell to the ground in a flailing, shouting heap.

After doing as much harm as two young boys could do to each other, they fell apart, exhausted. It was a draw. Meyer kept his pocket money and Charlie, eager to keep his dignity, decided to befriend his one-time target. He dubbed his new companion "Mighty Mite."

Meyer and Charlie were living proof that opposites attract. Meyer was small for his age, and even as an adult barely cleared five feet. Soft-spoken and discreet, he liked to fade into the background in the presence of others. He had a quick, mathematical mind, and though he left high school at age 14 and went to work in a machine shop, he was widely praised for his genius-level intelligence. The semi-literate Charlie would later refer to him, half-admiringly, half-disdainfully, as the "human adding machine." If he and Charlie had never met, he might have made a first-rate accountant. And without Meyer's planning and counsel — and an exceptionally foolish bit of legislation courtesy of the United States government — Charlie Lucania might always have remained a two-bit thug.

Prohibition: Noble Effort, Spectacular Failure

Since the late 1800s, there had been a growing concern among virtuous American citizens about the increase of alcohol abuse. Excessive drinking was blamed for rising crime rates, the decline in church attendance, and the resultant breakdown of social order. The so-called Temperance Movement strove to combat this vice by banning the sale of alcohol altogether.

In 1919, after years of unrelenting pressure from these special-interest groups, the government passed the infamous Volstead Act, popularly known as Prohibition. Overnight, it became illegal to manufacture, distribute, or sell liquor, except for medicinal purposes. Lawmen smashed wooden barrels of beer with hatchets, spilling their contents to the ground. Crates of alcohol were piled high then set ablaze in public view. Whatever remained was put under lock and key in government-owned warehouses.

Most citizens didn't share their government's view on the evils of drunkenness. It's doubtful, in fact, that a law has ever inspired such lawlessness. Before long, anything from bathtub gin to domestic beer to the finest French champagne was being smuggled into underground bars known as "speak-easies." People were more than willing to pay inflated prices for a drink. Vast fortunes were made overnight. Prohibition was a bootlegger's paradise.

Charlie Lucania was an ambitious young man. Though not a big drinker himself — he occasionally indulged in a glass or two of wine at the local Italian social clubs — he was quick to see the possibilities that Prohibition presented. When a friend named Joe Adonis offered to cut him in on a bootlegging scheme, he accepted without hesitation. For one of his first major deals, he found himself rumbling towards Philadelphia by train, his gun nestled in one pocket, a bundle of cash totaling $35,000 in the other. Charlie felt slightly giddy. It was probably the largest sum of money he had ever seen.

The life of a bootlegger offered all the money and excitement — and risk — he had ever desired. Though on this job he was only the bagman, or the tough guy carrying the cash, Charlie knew this was the life for him.

It was Meyer Lansky who pushed Charlie to take the operation to the next level. He advised his friend to think like a wholesaler, not a small-time hood. Instead of dealing with small shipments of booze from Canada and Scotland, he should do his utmost to corner the market. Meyer proposed that they also focus on the buyers. Instead of dealing alcohol diluted with water, or as was occasionally the case, turpentine, grain alcohol, and other poisonous substances, they would focus on acquiring the highest-quality merchandise and selling it to the classiest joints. They would be as businesslike and reliable as possible in order to attract and maintain a faithful clientele.

Soon they were successful beyond their wildest dreams. It cost $25 to purchase a crate of bootleg Scotch; they could resell it for over $1000. With the money they made, they rented several warehouses and purchased a fleet of trucks. They even owned printing presses to manufacture counterfeit labels for stolen bottles of booze. Theft was rampant in their business, so heavily armed men were always on hand, charged with protecting the precious cargo. And if they ever ran into trouble with the law, they had the top lawyers in the city only a phone call away. They even had an accounting division, charged with the daunting task of memorizing every financial transaction in order to eliminate a paper trail. In total, they employed over a hundred men in their organization. Charlie and his friends were moving into the upper echelons of crime. Though things were going well, it was a dangerous game they were playing.

With such huge sums of money to be made, there was always some hothead trying to hijack the merchandise or muscle in on their racket. The police, too, had a bad habit of showing up at the wrong time. While bullets took care of the first group, bribery took care of the second. Charlie and his gang were shameless in their dealings with the cops. Once, he and a friend were stopped for a traffic violation smack dab in the middle of the city with a cluster of shotguns and 45 rounds of ammo in the back of the car. When the officer asked what they were doing with the weapons, the bootlegger brazenly replied that they were hunting pheasants. He got off with a ticket — for driving without a license.

Sometimes, though, it seemed that the biggest threat to their cozy little setup was not nosy policemen or other gangsters. It was Charlie himself. Just when he appeared to be on top of the world, he was arrested yet again for possession of heroin.

Charlie was a big-time operator now. There was no need for someone in his position to dirty his hands with drug dealing. Though he denied it, and kept his drug problems well hidden from his associates, the most likely explanation is that the narcotics were for his personal use. In later years, lawmen would often include "drug addict" in a list of his crimes. Although he was able to bribe his way out of the charges against him, he was ordered to see a psychiatrist on a daily basis until he was deemed cured.

Following his arrest, Charlie endured a run of bad luck. First, a major shipment of booze was hijacked. Then, federal agents raided his warehouses. It would take months to recoup his losses. Unable to meet his commitments, Charlie reluctantly decided it was time to seek outside help.

The Men From Sicily

Charlie could see the writing on the wall. He was proud of the men he'd attracted to his service and the business they had created together. Moreover, he realized that the old-time gangs were too disorganized to ever be a real force and would soon be on their way out.

But Charlie remained as ambitious as ever, and he knew he had to find another way to survive. As the son of Sicilian immigrants, he had an "in" with one of the most powerful criminal organizations in the world. Ever since he was a boy, he had admired the distinguished-looking gentlemen who would occasionally make an entrance in his shabby, poverty-stricken neighborhood on the Lower East Side. They wore the finest tailored clothes, drove the grandest, most expensive cars, and had the most beautiful, glamorous women hanging on their arms. They were treated with respect bordering on reverence by the common people. Everyone jumped to attention when they spoke. These were the dons of the Mafia, the ancient, much-feared Sicilian crime families who had imported their criminal activities to American shores.

Ordinary Italian immigrants, like Charlie's parents, spoke of these men in hushed, fearful tones. Charlie suspected that his own father, once a worker in a sulfur mine in a dusty little village in Sicily, had entered into some kind of deal with the Mafia to finance his family's journey to America. He never knew for certain, though, as it would be indiscreet, even dangerous, to speak of such matters. His father, a dirt-poor laborer in his adopted country, had certainly cut any ties to the secret society.

Charlie had already been approached several times by Mafia operatives seeking to recruit him, but he had always politely refused. He preferred to be his own boss. But times were tough for the independent bootlegger. The secret society, he thought, could provide men, stability, and an unlimited bankroll for his illegal schemes. Charlie realized he had resisted their overtures long enough.

By the time the 1920s rolled around, Charlie was already viewed as something of a hot commodity by the leading Mafia dons. Though unschooled, he had an innate intelligence. While brutish in appearance, he had a discreet and respectful manner. Most importantly, he was willing to do anything — anything at all — to make money. If this meant selling narcotics, pimping young girls, and even committing murder, so be it. As far as Charlie was concerned, business was business.

It was Giuseppe Masseria, the self-styled leader of the U.S. Mafia, who finally convinced the budding gangster to work for him. Masseria rubbed his hands with glee when he thought of his new employee. Not only was the Lucania boy prized for his personal attributes, he would also bring with him the proceeds of a thriving criminal business. Masseria was not a subtle man. Impatient with Charlie's stalling, he finally clinched the deal by threatening to kill both Charlie and his partner, Joe Adonis, unless they joined up with him. "Now you have a chance to be my friends," their new boss said with a sinister smile, "or the both of you are dead men."

To Masseria's face, Charlie was polite, respectful, and attentive. The man they called "Joe the Boss" ate it up. This bright young man was exactly what was needed in his organization. Masseria was content to believe that his new protégé's arrest on drug charges was a minor glitch in an otherwise stellar career. One day, he promised, Charlie might even serve as his right-hand man — if he continued to do exactly what he was told, and promised to adhere to the ancient codes of the Mafia. Besides an unquestioning loyalty to the Boss, he explained, these codes included belief in the vendetta, or blood feud, and a reverence for personal and family honor. Without them, he swore, the Mafia was nothing.

Charlie played the part of the reverent Mafia soldier to perfection. To seal his entry into the society, the 25-year-old even gunned down one of Masseria's top rivals in broad daylight, in full view of dozens of terrified onlookers. Privately, though, he was disgusted by what he saw around him. Some of the codes of behavior, he thought, were silly and outmoded. He rolled his eyes at the secret handshakes and initiation rituals, and particularly shied away from the Sicilian habit of men kissing each other, either on the cheek as a greeting, or on the lips as a warning of impending danger. He also came to feel contempt for the old men who enforced such behavior. Though Masseria demanded that his underlings bow down before him, Charlie soon discovered that Joe the Boss was a stubborn, uncouth man, prone to violent outbursts. Cramming his mouth full of food, the fat little man would scream and curse at his henchmen, crumbs and spittle flying. Charlie considered him more worthy of contempt than respect.

Furthermore, as Charlie discovered, the sacred laws of the Mafia enforced by Masseria actually interfered with their ability to do business. It was forbidden to bribe the police, for example, as this was seen as conspiring with the enemy. (This didn't mean that it didn't happen, however. Charlie knew from past experience that if the men in blue weren't slipped a few bucks here and there to look the other way, he and his men were in constant danger of arrest and imprisonment. Without their boss's knowledge, one of Charlie's associates, a gun-toting tough named Frank Costello, born Francesco Castiglia, made an art of greasing palms to avoid arrest.)

Vendettas and infighting were also a threat to the stability of the organization. Don Masseria himself was so involved with his escalating dispute against his archrival, Salvatore

Maranzano, that he had barely enough time to oversee his own operations.

Allies, Enemies, and Victims

Another source of frustration for Charlie was the almost crazed racism many of the Mafiosi exhibited. Though Italians of non-Sicilian descent were tolerated — barely — as minor players in the organization, it was strictly forbidden to have business dealings with mobsters of any other ethnicity. This bothered Charlie to no end. Meyer Lansky, his best friend and long-time business associate, was a Jew and, despite his youth, was turning into one of the most able, intelligent criminals he'd ever encountered, in or out of the Mafia. Along with another Jewish friend, Benjamin "Bugsy" Siegel, Lansky was developing a powerful and lucrative enforcement outfit, trading muscle and firepower for cash. And there were many more local gangs, Jewish, Irish, and other, that would be profitable to cultivate.

The way Charlie saw it, there were only three kinds of people: allies, enemies, and victims. But Masseria saw red at the very whisper of an alliance, and demanded that his new recruit cut ties with his non-Italian associates. When Charlie broached the subject, Masseria roared that, as long as he was the *capo di tutti capi*, the boss of bosses, such deals with outsiders would never be.

A radical idea began to formulate in Charlie's mind. What if Masseria wasn't the supreme boss after all? The only alternative was his greatest enemy, Salvatore Maranzano. But Maranzano, a recent Italian immigrant, was even more unbending than Masseria. Neither of these powerful, unyielding men wanted outsiders intruding on what they liked to call the *Cosa Nostra*, Italian for "our thing."

Charlie and some of the other young Mafiosi had a secret name for these old-style Mafia leaders. They called them the "Mustache Petes" for the drooping facial hair many of them sported on their upper lips (although, ironically, both Masseria and Maranzano were clean shaven). What started as a joke among friends became a useful method of revealing the true feelings of Charlie's peers. Charlie noticed that anyone who laughed at the disrespectful nickname shared his view that the dons were hopelessly old-fashioned and out of date — expendable, even. Anyone who reacted with horror, on the other hand, was to be kept at arm's length. Charlie made a mental note of how everyone he worked with responded. Slowly, the list of potential allies grew longer and longer. Among those who sided with him were men who went on to become notorious in the annals of American crime: Frank Costello, Joe Adonis, Albert Anastasia, and Vito Genovese.

Charlie sentimentally referred to his band of killers and thieves as "the best team that ever got put together." By 1929, their numbers were so strong that they decided to call a summit of all the top criminals in the land — and not just those with Italian blood. Roughly half who turned up at the Atlantic City conference were members of Jewish gangs. Meyer Lansky, who had originated the idea of the conference, was there, along with all the top New York gangsters, including, of course, Charlie Lucania. Men known only as Boo-Boo and Greasy Thumb mixed with luminaries such as the famed Al Capone. Atlantic City was known as a party town and they certainly meant to enjoy themselves. For Lansky, this business trip was even doubling as his honeymoon. But before the booze, cigars, and showgirls were brought out, they had important matters to discuss.

After the men settled into their elegant suites at the Ritz, they assembled with the view of hammering out a business plan. To most of the men in attendance, these were radical new ideas they were discussing. But in truth, Charlie and Meyer Lansky had been dreaming of a new Syndicate for almost a decade. A hush fell over the room as they put forward their ideas. There would be a cross-country coalition of gangsters, they proposed, each with their own territory and interests. They would work with, not against, one another, regardless of their ethnic background. Unlike the vicious, war-like old-timers, they would get ahead using their brains, not just their guns. This would be a new era for the American underworld, they proclaimed, a time of unlimited power and prosperity.

But for the moment, this was all talk. Conspicuously absent from these discussions, and the convention itself, were the old-guard Mafiosi like Masseria and Maranzano. Nothing would ever change as long as such men continued to run the show. Of course, no one wanted to be the first to suggest a hit on such feared individuals. As the underworld conference disbanded, they decided to go for a more subtle approach.

Their plan was a cunning one. They would do nothing overt. Instead, they would pit Masseria and Maranzano against each other and allow them to destroy one another, leaving the top spot in the New York Mafia vacant. That way, none of them would be seen as traitors, inviting fatal retaliation from the supporters of those they had betrayed. Albert Anastasia, the tough longshoreman-turned-Mafia-killer, was so delighted by the plan that he flung his arms around its mastermind, Charlie Lucania, and enveloped him in a crushing hug. Despite his glee, it was a dangerous game that the secret confederates were about to set in motion.

Since the mid-1920s, Masseria and Maranzano had been at each other's throats. In 1928, open warfare at last broke out between the two. The bullets started flying and bodies were piling up in what became known as the "Castellammarese War," which took its name from Maranzano's home town of Castellammare del Golfo. But it was mostly the minor players who were being eliminated. Charlie now worked to speed things along, planting spies among Maranzano's men, and trying his hardest to sabotage the organization to which he himself belonged. He drove a wedge between the two bosses in another way, too: not only were they bickering over the prestigious title of "boss of bosses," they were also fiercely competing for the services of the increasingly powerful Charlie Lucania.

Maranzano, who had emerged as the more powerful of the two crime lords, covertly arranged a meeting with his rival's top man. His timing was impeccable. Though Charlie was secretly plotting the downfall of the bosses, he was still forced to work under them for the time being, and was increasingly unhappy with the situation. The greedy, violent-tempered Masseria was jealous of Charlie's prosperity and was demanding a greater-than-ever share in his earnings. The *capo* had set his eyes on Charlie's lucrative bootlegging profits, which had previously been off-limits. Furthermore, as a test of Charlie's loyalty, Masseria had recently forced his underling to actively participate in a bank robbery. Charlie was disgruntled, thinking it a job unbefitting to a rising star such as himself. He was management now, not muscle. To make matters worse, he had been caught red-handed during the caper — only some fast talking had gotten him off the hook. Keen to avoid a repeat of such an occurrence, he agreed to meet with the rival boss, despite his many reservations.

The meeting took place at the social club that doubled as Maranzano's unofficial office. His guest arrived alone and unarmed, though somewhat wary of taking a bullet in the back. Maranzano received him with open arms, however, and while several large, intimidating men with suspicious bulges under their arms made their presence felt, it soon became apparent that this was to be a straightforward business meeting, not an ambush. Maranzano poured out glasses of red wine and sentimentally called the younger man his *bambino*, or little boy, and chuckled over the fact that they shared the same first name, Salvatore. He confided that he might have a position — a very prominent position — for a young man of such immense talent.

The object of his flattery listened hard but said little, outwardly respectful as always. Though the condescending tone was not to his liking, and he had bridled at the unwelcome use of his real first name, Charlie found the offer itself tempting. He promised to give it the consideration it deserved. The two men shook hands and Charlie left to mull things over.

The next day, Charlie met with his closest confidants to discuss the matter. One by one, they urged him to accept the offer. They were convinced that, not only would it lead to more power and money, but the defection would so infuriate Masseria that a final, destructive war would be inevitable. There was only one voice of dissent. Lansky, with whom Charlie had been doing business all along, was also present. Having heard his friend's version of events and the advice of the other men, he finally offered his succinct opinion. "It stinks," was all he would say.

Kidnapped

Those two words uttered by Meyer Lansky would be enough to make anyone think twice. Days passed and Don Maranzano let it be known that he was increasingly anxious for an answer to his proposition. But still Charlie hesitated. In October of 1929, on the day the sleek black car with the curtained windows drew alongside him as he strolled down Sixth Avenue, it finally occurred to him: he had hesitated for too long.

Before Charlie could register what was happening, he found himself looking down the barrel of a gun. A couple of goons dragged him into the back of the vehicle and slammed the door behind him. His mouth was taped firmly shut and his wrists were roughly bound together as the car squealed off down the street. Too stunned to struggle, he had just enough time to register one thought before a well-aimed blow to the head knocked him unconscious: these weren't Maranzano's men after all. They worked for his own boss, Masseria.

When he finally regained consciousness, Charlie was shaking with fear. Even a killer with ice water in his veins dreads his own death. He found himself bound by the ankles, swinging upside down from the rafters in an abandoned warehouse. The smell of stale air and rat droppings filled his nostrils. Bright lights shone in his eyes, blinding and confusing him. Dizzy and disoriented, he barely registered the first blow. Soon, though, a flurry of fists descended on his vulnerable torso. How many men were attacking him, he had no way of knowing. The pounding force of their fists sent him swinging first to the right, then to the left, and finally spun him in juddering circles. Every available part of his body was punched, jabbed, kicked. Whenever he seemed to be on the verge of passing out, they burned his flesh with cigarettes to revive him.

Finally, someone produced a knife. Charlie's chest was hacked at, then the blade flashed downwards. The tip sunk into his face, just below his right eye, then moved down his cheek, slicing through muscle as it went. Blood dripped on the concrete floor. With that final, horrific act, the torture ended. The swaying body was cut down and bundled into the back of a waiting car.

Chapter 2 The Birth of Lucky Luciano

It was just another late-night shift for the two officers cruising the Staten Island beat. The men chatted quietly as the squad car rolled through the damp, darkened streets. A little after 2 a.m., their headlights picked out a crumpled form by the side of the road, and the cruiser slid to a stop. A drunk sleeping it off, they suspected, or, even more likely, a victim of the escalating mob wars. Like some, the cops might have privately cheered at the thought of criminals methodically destroying each other — as long as innocent civilians weren't involved.

Whatever the case, they were in no hurry as they stepped from the car, stretched, and strolled over to the prone figure. It was immediately clear that this was no drunk in a stupor. The dead man's tweed suit, while soiled, was of the finest quality, and his hair, though stiff with blood, was expensively cut and groomed. This was clearly a Mob traitor, taken for the "long ride" — the one-way trip from which no one ever returned. As one officer radioed in a report of the murder, the other leaned in to get a better view of the corpse. His startled shout rang out when the "corpse" moaned and slowly sat up, its face a mask of blood. The leisurely call to headquarters became a frantic race to the nearest hospital. The partners hoisted the bloodied figure into the rear of the cruiser and, sirens wailing, tore off through the starlit night.

The cops were no fools. This had to be big. Even before they reached the emergency room, they began to pump their battered cargo for information. They were convinced he was a member of the Mafia — his voice even retained a faint hint of an Italian accent. And he was clearly one of the higher-ups — his expensive clothing told them that. But what had he done to betray the organization? And who exactly had administered such a cruel beating? The individual slumped over in the back seat wouldn't talk. Though he reluctantly gasped out his name, Charles Luciano, he would say little else.

The police continued to badger Charlie even after doctors had stitched him up and pronounced him fit enough to return home. It hadn't taken them long to realize that this Charles Luciano was the same Salvatore Lucania they had encountered countless times before; he had unofficially changed his name for its easier pronunciation. No matter how hard the cops probed him, he continued to confound them with silence or evasive answers. He stared at the floor and mumbled repeatedly that he was an innocent victim with no ties to the Mafia at all. The more he tried to deny it, the more certain the police were that he knew exactly who the perpetrators were. They grilled him for hours, asking the same questions again and again. Finally, Charlie had enough. The cops should just lay off him, he snarled. He would take care of the matter himself.

There is little the law can do in these circumstances. Out of sheer annoyance at Charlie's stubbornness, the police arrested him with an obviously trumped-up accusation of grand theft auto, though the charge, as usual, was immediately dropped. Eventually, they abandoned the investigation altogether, citing lack of evidence and a very uncooperative victim. No one was ever arrested for the sadistic crime. That did not mean, however, that it went unpunished.

In a matter of days, Charlie was back on his feet and frequenting his old haunts — the cafes, brothels, and street corners where men of his type congregated. His friends were stunned by his appearance. With his coarse, pockmarked features, Charlie had never been a beauty queen, but now his bruised and swollen face was a terrible sight. A row of stitches — over 50 of them — adorned his cheek. One eye had a permanent droop to it, a result of nerve damage. Most of his injuries, the cuts and the burn marks, were hidden under his clothing. The only clue he gave to the amount of pain he was in was his excessively careful movements. He moved as slowly and gingerly as an old man. But his spirit was fierier than ever.

Word quickly got around that Charlie Luciano had been taken for the long ride — and lived. Some naysayers hinted that the story was a cover-up for a botched drug deal, even a kidnapping, or that a gang of rogue cops had decided to teach him a lesson. Others insisted it was Maranzano who had ordered the beating, out of frustration at Charlie's refusal to join forces with him. Nevertheless, the fact that he was still standing after such a vicious assault gave him a legendary, almost superhuman status among his Mafia brothers. No matter what the odds, he seemed always to emerge a winner. From now on, the former Salvatore Lucania would be called "Lucky" by friend and enemy alike.

The man who had orchestrated the brutal attack, however, would be considerably less fortunate. Lucky's dislike for the perpetrator had turned into full-blown hatred. The Mafia notions of personal honor and bloody vengeance he had sneered at before now seemed very real to him. The old plan, to stand aside until the Mustache Petes eliminated each other, was no longer satisfying. Through cracked, swollen lips, he pressed for a bold new strategy. Lucky had committed murder before. This would be his first assassination.

Incident at the Villa Nuova

On the morning of April 15, 1931, Lucky approached his target, smiling and respectful as always to his superior's face. Joe the Boss Masseria smiled back, suspecting nothing. Lucky had been a changed man since their little misunderstanding, humble and deferential. Masseria, a crafty, paranoid individual who had already survived several attempts on his life, had somehow been lulled into complacency. A year and a half had passed since he'd ordered the attack; Masseria was certain he had nothing more to fear from the man he had tried to kill. When his underling proposed a trip to Coney Island for lunch and a relaxing game of cards, he was delighted to accept. Lucky suggested the Nuova Villa Tammaro, a cozy Italian establishment where Joe the Boss felt particularly at home — the owner, Gerardo Scarpato, was an old friend of his. It would be a pleasant break from the rigors of running one of the biggest criminal organizations in the country.

Masseria, whose piggish manners had always disgusted Lucky, was in fine form that pleasant spring day. He ladled huge forkfuls of pasta into his mouth, spattering his shirt and tie with clam sauce, and guzzled bottle after bottle of red wine. He so enjoyed his three-hour meal that he failed to notice the other diners stealing out the door, one by one. Even his friend, the restaurateur Scarpato, slipped out to take a conveniently timed walk along the beach. Red-faced and rather drunk, Masseria followed the meal with a few hands of cards with his second-in-command. They chatted idly while they sipped their espressos. At roughly half past three, Lucky scraped back his chair and excused himself to go to the washroom, leaving his boss alone at the cloth-covered table.

But not for long. With a crash, the door to the Villa Nuova was flung open, and four armed men burst in.

Masseria would have recognized them instantly. Three of them, he saw, were his own men. There was cocky Joe Adonis, who had inducted Lucky Luciano into the bootlegging trade. Beside him stood Albert Anastasia, also known as the Mad Hatter, a self-proclaimed "loudmouthed bum," notorious for having been paroled from prison while he was on death row. And there was lantern-jawed Vito Genovese, a man Lucky claimed to trust implicitly but could never bring himself to like.

The thought that the three of them were there with an urgent message for him might have flashed through Masseria's wine-fogged mind. What could be so important that they would disrupt his lunch hour in such a fashion? But the sight of the fourth intruder, a man he would have known by reputation alone, would have transformed his puzzlement to fear and outrage. It was Bugsy Siegel, the dapper, blue-eyed thug who, along with Lucky's old pal Meyer Lansky, headed the vicious Bug and Meyer Mob. Masseria nearly jumped out of his seat. His men were forbidden to deal with Jewish criminals like Siegel. This could only mean trouble.

Masseria wasn't given the chance to protest. The assassins wasted no time pumping six shots into his corpulent frame. He fell backwards with a crash onto the wooden floor, blood spurting, the ace of clubs still clutched in his out-flung hand. His killers checked for a pulse and, finding none, vanished as quickly as they came, leaving nothing behind but their bloody footprints.

The mastermind behind the hit emerged from his hiding place and looked down in satisfaction at what his men had accomplished. In an audacious move, Lucky himself then phoned the police to report the murder, and patiently waited until the squad cars showed up. It was immediately obvious that this was a Mob hit — and equally obvious who had ordered it.

Though the police pressed him hard, Lucky wouldn't give an inch. He pointed out that he had been "in the can" washing his hands when the bullets started to fly, and could therefore rightly claim that he hadn't actually been a witness to the murder. Amazingly, the ploy worked. With no additional witnesses — at least none willing to step forward — the police were forced to relinquish the man they strongly suspected had orchestrated the elaborate murder plot. Once again, Lucky got off scot-free.

Masseria's funeral was a solemn affair. Floral tributes and heartfelt speeches were the order of the day. Front and center at the service was Lucky Luciano, weeping a few crocodile tears over the untimely death of his mentor. And then there was Salvatore Maranzano, Masseria's old enemy, expressing his boundless sorrow at the tragedy. That, too, was a sham. Both men had benefited enormously from Masseria's demise.

The King of New York

With the death of Joe the Boss, the Castellammarese War was effectively over. Maranzano announced that an elegant banquet would be held in honor of the truce. The top Mafiosi were invited to attend, 500 of them in all. A throne was reportedly rented for the event. On it sat Maranzano, looking down on his new subjects, graciously accepting the cash-stuffed envelopes they had brought with them. Seated on his immediate right, smiling but watchful, was Lucky Luciano.

As the gangsters settled, Maranzano waved his hand for silence. His first order of business would be to pardon all the acts of violence that had taken place during the war. The vendetta was over. There would be no further retaliation for past crimes. Many in his audience were relieved to hear this news, while others were offended by his lordly tone.

Other changes would be made, Maranzano announced. True, these changes would involve some minor restructuring of the organization, but it was all for the best. The City of New York would be divided into five sections. Each section would be run by individual crime families, separate but equal to each other. One of these five families, the one formerly led by the dear departed Giuseppe Masseria, would be led by that able young man they all knew, Charles Luciano. Everyone knew he had been responsible for the other man's death, but still they applauded the news.

Maranzano wasn't finished. Most importantly, he stated, they would now answer to a new boss of bosses — Maranzano himself. Henceforth, his word would be law. Second in command in the chain of power would again be Lucky. As he wound up his speech, he emphasized that, despite the personnel shuffle, all the old rules still applied. For the good of the entire outfit, all members had to swear to uphold the traditions of the Mafia, which had lately come under attack. Glasses were raised and cheers filled the air. Maranzano beamed from his lofty seat, confident he had won over the crowd and nipped any dissent in the bud.

Lucky, not surprisingly, was quick to pledge his support to the aging don. The envelope he presented in tribute was stuffed with $50,000 cash to prove it. But in private, both men were singing a different tune. Lucky was still secretly scheming to eradicate the backward-looking Mustache Petes, embodied by the new *capo*, Salvatore Maranzano. And Maranzano was intelligent enough to realize that, given the opportunity, Lucky would destroy him without blinking an eye. Though the Masseria assassination had given him ultimate power, it also showed him how vulnerable the exalted position was. Perhaps a stool pigeon had whispered the treacherous details of the Atlantic City conference in his ear as well. Lucky, in any case, was a greater threat to him than ever before, and would have to be swatted down like a fly. Until he was gone, there could be no peace.

A contract was put out on Lucky and three of his top allies. The targets included two of the shooters in the Masseria assassination — Genovese and Adonis. The fourth victim was to be another of Lucky's long-time business associates, Frank Costello. The hit was assigned to the appropriately named Vincent "Mad Dog" Coll. For $50,000, Mad Dog, working alone, was entrusted with the task of killing four of the most dangerous men in America.

The plot against Lucky and his men had none of the artistic flourishes that characterized Masseria's assassination. Lucky and his lieutenant, Genovese, would be summoned to Maranzano's office for a routine meeting. Once there, they would be welcomed by the new receptionist, Mad Dog Coll. The unsuspecting twosome would be pumped full of lead before they could reach for their own guns. Their bullet-ridden bodies would be transported to a secondary site and hidden there so well that it would be weeks, possibly even years, before their decaying corpses were found.

The call came on September 10, 1931, only five months after the death of Masseria. As planned, Lucky and Genovese were asked to attend an afternoon meeting at Maranzano's Park Avenue office suite. They were told to show up at 2 p.m. sharp to discuss an important matter. The great man sat at his desk digesting his lunch as five burly, well-armed bodyguards stood protectively around him. Mad Dog would be there any minute. The trap was set.

Fifteen minutes before the appointed time, a tapping sounded at the door. To Maranzano's surprise, his receptionist led in one of his faithful employees, Tommy Lucchese. Only five foot two and missing a finger on one hand, Tommy struck most people as a harmless, agreeable little fellow. Those who knew him knew better. Tommy had a reputation in the organization as a ruthless and efficient killer. Maranzano's bodyguards wisely surrounded him and frisked him to make sure he was unarmed. After a quick pat-down, they announced that he was clean. Nevertheless, he was suspiciously hazy when they roughly demanded why he was there. No one knew what to make of it.

Tommy, of course, was moonlighting as a spy for Lucky. He had informed Lucky of the conspiracy almost as soon as it had been hatched, leaving plenty of time to devise a cunning counterplot. His purpose in arriving at the office prior to the meeting time was to ensure everything went according to plan.

Moments after Tommy's surprise appearance, four official-looking men in drab suits strode into the office. Their arrival was even less welcome than Tommy's. Holding their badges aloft, they announced they were government agents with questions regarding Maranzano's back taxes. The don nonchalantly waved them in.

While the Mob could easily shrug off charges of fraud, battery, extortion, even murder, it had an Achilles heel: the Internal Revenue Service (IRS). Down in Chicago, Al Capone was being pursued by the crime-busting team known as the Untouchables, led by the famed Eliot Ness. When all other avenues failed, they would eventually bring Capone down by proving he had paid virtually no taxes on the millions he made in the illegal liquor trade. Though it was a minor infraction compared to his other crimes, it was the only charge brought against him that would stick. Maranzano was thus as polite and accommodating to his four guests as he could be, despite the beads of sweat collecting on his brow. The bodyguards didn't even bother to search them.

Then, at a sign from Tommy Lucchese, the interlopers dropped their charade and pulled out their guns. They weren't lawmen, they were hit men — Jewish gangsters hired specifically for their ethnicity. Lucky had reasoned that four Italians pretending to work for the government would have aroused too much suspicion. The ruse worked. Two of the men overpowered Maranzano effortlessly, frog-marching him out of the reception area and into his private office. Tommy and the other two subdued the receptionist and bodyguards, holding them at gunpoint and threatening to shoot them if they so much as made a sound.

After slamming the office door behind them, Maranzano's captors pocketed their guns. The don felt a glimmer of hope — maybe they didn't mean to kill him, after all — until he saw the lethal blades glittering in their hands. Gunshots would make too much noise echoing through a busy office building. Knife wounds, on the other hand, are as silent as they are deadly.

Maranzano fought off the attack as fiercely as he could. Though he was stabbed six times, including once directly to the throat, he refused to back down. Gasping for breath, dripping with blood, he swung empty-handed at his attackers, desperately trying to protect himself. Finally, in frustration, the hit men pocketed their blood-stained knives and pulled out their handguns once more. A shot rang out, then three more, and Salvatore Maranzano collapsed onto the office floor.

Tommy and his four cohorts fled the scene, with the bodyguards in hot pursuit. One of the bodyguards gave up the chase when he saw a familiar figure entering the building. It was Mad Dog Coll, on his way to kill Lucky and Genovese. When Mad Dog heard what had transpired, he decided to make himself scarce. Half of his $50,000 fee had been paid in advance, and he had no intention of trying to collect the rest. To do so would be to sign his own death warrant. He walked away untroubled, whistling a happy tune.

Genovese and Lucky never made it to their afternoon appointment with Maranzano. Even Lucky, with all his good luck, knew that being present at the murders of two crime lords in under six months would bring the entire NYPD down on his back, hard. The two were far away, letting themselves be seen, establishing an alibi. Besides, they were busy.

The Rise of the Unione Siciliane

It was a bloodbath, insiders said. Lucky Luciano, in a bid to eliminate the last of the Mustache Petes, had dozens of old-guard Mafiosi eliminated in one final strike. In Mafia lore, the day of Maranzano's murder was given a chilling name, "The

Night of the Italian Vespers." The story, while enticingly gory, is not strictly true. Lucky himself publicly scoffed at such a far-fetched idea. The only other confirmed Mafia-related murder on that day was that of Gerardo Scarpato, owner of the Nuova Villa Tammaro, the man who had permitted his friend Giuseppe Masseria to be slaughtered under his nose. A few remaining hardliners did meet unfortunate ends in the days following the death of Maranzano, but most of them had been strategically killed off during the Castellammarese War. That day in September was hardly the bloodbath the rumors indicated. Lucky Luciano was so respected and feared that few stood in his way.

Following Maranzano's stately, well-attended funeral, Lucky requested another general meeting of the top criminals in the land. Like the Atlantic City conference, it would include mobsters of all ethnicities. They met in Chicago this time. Lucky was slightly uncomfortable in the crime-ridden city he dismissed as a "crazy place," but no one noticed his unease. There were so many attendees that they overran two hotels. The halls and lobbies buzzed with excitement. One of the big topics of conversation was the approaching end of the bootlegging trade. It was becoming clear that the government was on the verge of abandoning Prohibition. Such an act would spell financial disaster for them all. Everyone was eager to hear what Lucky had to say.

Rising to his feet in the center of the packed (and carefully guarded) conference room, Lucky began to speak. The events of the past few months had been unpleasant, but necessary, he said. Certain individuals, whom he delicately refrained from naming, had stood in the way of the success of their little operation. Now that they were gone, it was time for other, more accomplished men to take over. He suggested that, as successful businessmen, they must all maintain their independence. Yet, in order to remain strong, they must also somehow unite. He suggested that they abandon the term "Mafia" and join together under a new name: the "Unione Siciliane." Despite the Italian name, any able man could be a part of the new venture. Those of other ethnicities would, by joining, become honorary Sicilians. There would be equal rights for all.

It would be a business, first and foremost. Under the old system, they had been subject to the whims of the *capo*. Now they would answer to a board of directors, Lucky explained, as Meyer Lansky nodded his approval in the background. Should anyone disapprove of his boss's orders or actions, he could appeal to the board for a ruling on the matter. And there would be no more infighting among the various groups. Everyone, including the public, was getting tired of the unnecessary bloodshed, he pointed out to murmurs of agreement. And what would they do without the huge profits reaped from the illegal sale of booze? Lucky laughed off their concerns. He pointed out that, by establishing ties with legitimate overseas distilleries, they could easily move into the legal business of importing alcohol once the Volstead Act was repealed. Furthermore, with their newfound strength they could branch out in all sorts of profitable directions. Gambling, in particular, was the way of the future. No one had anything to worry about.

Then, to the amazement of his listeners, Lucky did the unthinkable: he abolished the role of boss of bosses. Even his supporters had suspected he was chasing that prize. Though they all clutched their envelopes stuffed with tribute money, Lucky told them to put them away. "I got plenty," he laughed, "and besides, why should you be payin' anythin' to me when we're all equals?"

Admittedly, the board of directors was stacked with Lucky's cronies, and it was very clear they considered his word law. Lucky would be *capo* despite what he said. But the new system was still loudly applauded. Old-timers appreciated the name Unione Siciliane, a tip of the hat to the old days. The new guard were excited by the freedom the alliance would bring. Mostly, though, their thoughts turned to the enormous profits they would share under the banner of the Unione. No longer were they warring outfits divided along ethnic lines. They had become, almost overnight, a powerful, cross-country network of criminals. Their income would soon outstrip many of the top legitimate businesses in the country. And it was all thanks to one man: Lucky Luciano.

Chapter 3
Living the High Life at the Height of the Depression

On October 29, 1929, the United States was racked by the biggest financial disaster in its history: the stock market crash. All across the country businesses failed, homes were repossessed, and families declared bankruptcy while their children went hungry. It was a time of poverty and soup kitchens, bread lines and want. But for a select group of businessmen, whose strength lay in exploiting the weakness of others, the Depression was a time of opportunity and advancement. Their CEO was Lucky Luciano.

Despite his modest refusal of the title of *capo di tutti capi,* everyone knew who was really in charge of the restructured Mafia, popularly known as the Syndicate. To Lucky, in fact, the name "Unione Siciliane" was something of an embarrassment. He actually preferred the term "the outfit," but had as usual heeded the advice of the man he could now openly refer to as his *consigliere,* or top advisor. It was Meyer Lansky, always thinking ahead, who had persuaded him to throw the hard-core Mafia types a bone. "A lot of these guys need something to believe in," Meyer explained to his friend.

With Lucky now in charge of the outfit, they soon rebounded from the stock market crash. True, they had to adjust the scope of their operations. With money so tight, the average man on the street didn't carry around huge wads of cash in his pocket anymore. But he likely did still carry a few loose coins, and it was these small sums that the outfit now targeted. From penny lotteries to slot machines, small change equaled big bucks for the Unione.

Another money-making scheme lay in infiltrating legitimate businesses. Much as bootlegging had been a foot in the door with regards to the legal import/export business, loan-sharking gave the Mob a hold over genuine tradespeople. When borrowers failed to pay off the inflated interest rates on the loans they took out, they had two unpleasant options. Either hand over the reins or face, at best, a beating. At worst, they might show up at work one morning to find the place had been bombed to the ground. It was the same racket that Lucky had run as a young boy, extorting pennies from his schoolmates, but with far more dangerous consequences for his victims. Rather than face ruin, most borrowers reluctantly agreed to cooperate.

It was estimated that, at the height of the outfit's influence, even the most law-abiding American citizen would come into daily contact with at least one item that was tainted by Mob control. Almost everything, from groceries to newspapers to the very clothes people wore on their backs, was funded or controlled by organized crime.

As the unofficial boss of bosses, Lucky had a finger in every pie. No matter how lowly the operation, a percentage of the profits would trickle up to him. He liked to boast that his outfit was one of the biggest industries in the country, on par with General Motors. The Mob leader was on his way to becoming one of the richest and most powerful men in the land, and he was careful to look the part.

Ever since Lucky's teenage days working in the garment industry, he had been obsessed with fashion. As soon as his income allowed, he began to invest in his appearance. His shoes were hand-tooled leather, his suits tailor-made. His shirts and underwear were of the finest silk, and were hand-embroidered with his initials. But he was careful not to be too flashy. He thought Al Capone and the other Chicago gangsters were a little cartoonish, with their loud suits and boldly patterned ties. Lucky admonished his men not to be "crumbs," but to dress conservatively and behave responsibly. He himself was careful to cultivate a sober, businesslike image. The only extravagance he permitted in his appearance was the discreet diamond ring he wore on his little finger.

Lucky made other attempts to stay low-key. He was curiously law-abiding — he never let a parking ticket go unpaid. He rented his luxurious apartment at the exclusive Waldorf Astoria under an assumed name, Charles Ross, and unfailingly paid the $800 rent on the first of the month, in cash. The place doubled as an office space, his working hours stretching from midnight until dawn. People would drop by to receive instructions, ask for favors, or just shoot the breeze. A monthly bribe assuaged any concerns the manager might have had about some of the less savory characters who came to visit Lucky there.

In many ways the Mob boss was a simple man. He enjoyed trips to the ice cream parlor and laughing at the antics of the top comedians of the day. A night at the movies was a favorite treat, and in his spare time he enjoyed tinkering with the engines of the fleet of luxury cars he owned. During New York's harsh winter months, he took time off to sun himself on the beaches of Florida. Life, for the unrepentant criminal, was good. But Lucky found it difficult to resist a few of the flashier temptations that came with his high-profile lifestyle.

Ever since his bootlegging days, Lucky had moved on the periphery of high society. As the purveyor of high-quality hooch, he had the best seat in the house at the city's top night spots. Jaded chorus girls and breathless debutantes alike threw themselves at him. Fashionable people were eager to be seen in his company. Once he had ascended to the top of the Mob hierarchy, he was invited to play golf with them, toasting their health at members-only clubs and spending weekends at their country retreats. At the racetrack, he and his guests relaxed in his private box. With such an intense social schedule, it became increasingly difficult to maintain a low profile.

The crime lord reveled in his newfound celebrity. His smiling face with its sinister cast was photographed at parties, and the gossip columns were studded with his name. Many in the upper reaches of the social stratosphere were thrilled to be associated with a known criminal. Others were outraged at his impertinent behavior. One time a reporter approached him at a function and challenged him to reveal his real occupation. Years of dealing with the police had provided Lucky with the perfect answer. "Professional gambler," he said with a broad grin.

The climax of Lucky's public life was probably the night of the heavyweight championships. All across the city, people were clamoring for tickets to the sold-out show, but there were none to be had. Lucky had some influence in the boxing world. Like most gangsters of note, he owned a "piece" of an up-and-comer. Applying a little gentle pressure, he persuaded the promoters to find 200 spare seats in the house. Soon, the city's best and brightest were lining up at his door, begging for favors. He carefully hand-picked those who would attend the bout. "We hadda go with the best," he boasted.

Excitement hung in the air the evening of the big fight, as tangible as the musk of the women's perfumes and the smoke from the men's cigars. Everyone was dressed to the nines, including their beaming host. Lucky moved among New York's glitterati, preening and posing. He had dressed the part, his usual immaculate suit set off by a tie spotted with tiny horseshoes. The fight itself was almost secondary. Everybody wanted to be seen with the notorious gangster, to slap his back, shake his hand, or have their photo taken with him by eager lensmen. That night, Lucky Luciano was king.

The Making of an Empire

In his private dealings, Lucky was becoming equally bold. His days as an independent bootlegger had taught him that the criminal's greatest friend was a cop on the take. His friend Frank Costello, sometimes known as the prime minister of the organization, had educated him in the art of greasing palms. It was without a doubt the smartest way of assuring that business would be conducted unhindered. There were plenty of takers. At the time, police corruption was rampant, not just in New York, but in police forces across the country. From the lowliest beat cop to the highest-ranking officers, there was always someone willing to look the other way in exchange for a few dollars.

To this end, one of the new *capo's* first acts was to abolish the most frustrating of the old Mafia rules: no handouts to cops. Once he was in power, bribery escalated to dizzying heights. Once a week, a courier would visit the office of the police commissioner with a paper sack discreetly tucked under his arm. In the sack was a tidy stack of bills, amounting to as much as $20,000. No one ever dared to stop the courier as he went about his business, though Lucky instructed him to pretend to change a light bulb every once in a while, to blend in.

The total monthly expenditure on bribes amounted to many thousands of dollars, but this was a pittance compared to the tax-free millions the outfit was pulling in. Soon, everyone wanted a piece of the action.

From 1930 to 1931, New Yorkers saw a marvel of engineering, the Empire State Building, spring up before their eyes. For decades, it was the tallest building on the continent. But at the same time that this wonder of the modern world was being erected, corruption was threatening to tear down another New York institution. It was whispered that the couriers with their innocuous paper bags had begun visiting city hall as well. The public's love affair with high-flying criminals began to wane. They were less than thrilled to see their elected officials in bed with thieves and murderers. Mayor Jimmy Walker was rumored to be deep in the Mob's pocket. The outcry from the media and citizenry when this was discovered was so great that Walker eventually left office under a dark cloud of suspicion in 1932.

But the corruption didn't end there. The outfit would go to great lengths to put an end to official meddling. Candidates for state or federal positions often found financing from very dubious sources. Republican or Democrat, the Syndicate didn't care, as long as they promised to ease things along for their sinister backers. Lucky claimed that the rot spread to the highest echelons of power. "I don't say we elected Roosevelt," he smirked, "but we gave him a pretty good push."

Adding fuel to the public's outrage were the activities of a Brooklyn-based branch of the Unione Siciliane. Led by a rotating group, including Lucky's old pals Albert Anastasia and Joe Adonis, and a third man, "Judge" Louis Lepke, the offshoot was dubbed "Murder, Incorporated" by the media for the businesslike way they dispatched their prey. To be accurate, Murder, Inc. was an in-house organization only. Its members were strictly forbidden to kill outsiders — at least not without the authorization of the Unione's board of directors.

Until an informer brought it to its knees in 1940, Murder, Inc.'s hit men ruthlessly dispatched anywhere from 500 to 1000 victims. Their methods were as creative as they were lethal. Death could come quickly, via a bullet to the brain, an ice pick jabbed straight into the heart, or a garrote tightly wound around an unsuspecting victim's neck. But there were also more elaborate methods of elimination. One unlucky thief who stole coins from a Mob-owned slot machine found himself strapped to that very machine moments before being dumped in a lake. And in one of the most famous incidents in the history of the Mafia, a stool pigeon under police protection was thrown from the window of a 75-foot building — as his supposed protectors sat idly in an adjacent room.

In many ways, this efficient killing was more frightening than the shoot-'em-ups of the bootlegging era. The public began to realize that mobsters weren't the daring outlaws of the movies, but cold, amoral killers who would do anything to make a buck.

Public officials began to pay attention. The new mayor of New York, Fiorello La Guardia, ordered the reluctant police commissioner to crack down on organized crime. The mayor ushered in the new era by rounding up the city's illegally operated slot machines and dumping them in the river. Corruption, however, was so deeply ingrained that only a few other cosmetic changes were made. It's true, the men in blue did start to bring more gangsters in for questioning, but it was hardly a crackdown. The suspected criminals were chauffeured to and from their homes by police drivers and, once down at the station, were faced with little more than apologies and pleasantries. The number of actual arrests scarcely increased at all.

This changed with the arrival of a special prosecutor named Thomas Dewey. Dewey was a one-man crusader against crime, the Eliot Ness of New York State. When the district attorney's office had proved ineffectual in the fight against the Mob, Dewey had received authorization from a grand jury to go after organized crime on a large scale, all by himself. No one in the Syndicate liked the attention the little man with the big mustache was focusing on their operation. They were further dismayed when they discovered that Dewey, like La Guardia, could not be bought off. He would be coming after them, like it or not.

The special prosecutor's first target was Dutch Schultz, the former bootlegging legend who had moved into the numbers racket in a big way. Like Al Capone, Schultz was first targeted for income tax evasion, before the more serious charges of racketeering and murder were brought against him. Schultz was so incensed by the persecution he was suffering that, while out on bail, he approached the Unione's board of directors with a shocking proposition.

One of the few Mafia rules adopted by the Syndicate had been the one forbidding the execution of outsiders. Schultz argued that he was in such danger that an exception would have to be made. The board of directors was understandably reluctant to carry out such a risky business, even if it meant one of their own ended up in jail. Nevertheless, the first steps were taken. Dewey's home was staked out, his comings and goings monitored. The site of the hit, it was decided, would be the pharmacy where he stopped every morning on his way to work. A hit man was reportedly chosen: career criminal Albert Anastasia, the sometime leader of Murder, Inc. Everything was planned down to the last detail. Then, only days before the murder was to occur, the unthinkable happened. Anastasia was told to put away his gun. Lucky Luciano had personally called off the hit.

Dutch Schultz blew up. He had always been a lone wolf, likely the reason he, not the less-vulnerable Lucky, had been targeted. When the Unione withdrew its support, Schultz threatened to carry out the hit himself. The board of directors met again, in a back room at one of the Jewish delicatessens that Lucky had become fond of. This time, however, Schultz was noticeably absent. Someone was posing a major threat to the organization, the council agreed. An assassination was imperative. But the special prosecutor wouldn't be the target, as previously planned. It would be their old friend and colleague, Dutch Schultz.

The former bootlegger was considered a loose cannon by the top Mafia executives. Once he was behind bars, there was no telling what he would do — or, more importantly, say. Many of the board members had a personal dislike of the man as well. Lucky had a particular distaste for Schultz, complaining that among his other personal shortcomings, he "dressed like a pig," which might have been a factor in their decision. On the other hand, Dutch knew how to make himself useful. It was he who had ordered the execution of Mad Dog Coll, the hit man who was to have hunted down and killed Lucky, Schultz himself, and countless others. But this was taken as another sign of his unpredictable nature.

Dewey, in contrast, was considered an essentially harmless nuisance. Though it was likely Dewey would make Lucky his target once Schultz was removed from the picture, Lucky was confident he could beat any rap brought against him.

Since taking over the top spot, Lucky had taken care to avoid direct involvement in any crime. Gone were the days when he might provide extra muscle during a bank robbery, or sell a little dope with the hopes of skimming a few grams off the top for his own use. He had little sympathy left for people like Dutch who put their own interests above the good of the outfit. On October 23, 1935, two gunmen entered the Palace Chop House in Newark, New Jersey, where Schultz was dining with three companions, and shot the entire party dead. It was the most important Mob hit since the murders of Masseria and Maranzano nearly five years earlier, and it turned the attention of the media — and the law — straight to Lucky.

Unbeknownst to Lucky, his activities were already being monitored. His phone was tapped and his movements were watched by covert operators. Lucky had always taken care in covering his tracks. He was now so discreet that he'd even begun using a code name, "3-12" (the third and twelfth letters of the alphabet — his initials), in his phone conversations, in case anyone was listening in.

In Lucky's mind, he was in the clear. They couldn't nail him for tax evasion — as a "professional gambler," he always declared his modest annual income of $25,000. They couldn't nail him for murder — he was so high up in the chain of command it would be impossible to trace such acts back to him. The evidence for his older crimes, such as robbery, bootlegging, and the like, had been swept under the carpet by a cooperative police force. It would take a miracle to pin anything on him. A miracle or, as he would later complain, a conspiracy.

Dewey's Trail of Vice

As one of the few females working in the office of the district attorney, Eunice Carter was given all the lowly women's work. For the assistant D.A., this meant that "social" crimes like prostitution were her specialty, whether she liked it or not. It was doubtful she would ever be permitted to work on any of the more important files that passed through the D.A.'s office. What was worse, when she reported that a strange pattern was emerging in the stories told by the "working girls" she dealt with, her suspicions were laughed away by the men she worked for.

It was clear to Carter that there was a significant connection between many of the prostitutes she interviewed. Under interrogation, they almost always told the same story. They were innocent small-town girls, new to the big city, who happened to be in the wrong place at the wrong time. It was as though someone had instructed them beforehand in the art of gaining a jury's sympathy. In court, lawyers from the same firm would turn up to defend them. Fines and bail money always came from the same hands. And the charges against them were being dropped at a suspiciously high rate.

To Carter, all this strongly suggested that some unknown person had, in the past two or three years, started organizing the brothel workers and streetwalkers. Only one group of people had the know-how to organize crime on such a grand scale. It was clear to her that the Mafia had moved in on the flesh-peddling trade. When her superiors continued to turn a blind eye to her findings, she decided to contact the man who was building a reputation for fighting such criminals — Thomas Dewey.

The special prosecutor was the only one who would hear her out. He listened to her story and became so convinced she was on to something that he encouraged her to leave the D.A.'s office to work for him full-time. Gradually, they uncovered more evidence of a centrally operated prostitution ring, enough to warrant a major crackdown on the city's houses of ill repute.

In early 1936, Eunice Carter's work with Thomas Dewey led to the arrest of over 100 pimps. Madams and call girls were arrested in a series of raids on 41 different brothels throughout New York City. Investigators eagerly sought the name of the ringleader. Though most prisoners initially pointed to a circle of small-time pimps with casual ties to the Mafia, they were quick to pick up on their interrogators' interest in one specific name. At the mention of the well-known crime lord, Lucky Luciano, Dewey nearly began to salivate.

Slowly, Dewey and his assistants began to piece together a case against Lucky. The Depression had hit the outfit hard, they theorized. In order to maintain his lavish lifestyle, Lucky had commanded his underlings to take pimping, the lowliest of crimes in the eyes of the Mafia, into the big time. Besides their usual 50 percent cut, the pimps charged the girls a weekly fee in exchange for food, shelter, and protection. On top of that was an exorbitant "booking fee" if the girls wanted to keep working. It was more akin to extortion than pandering. Anyone who refused to cooperate would have her eyes blackened or her front teeth knocked out. One unfortunate who defied them took a blow from a lead pipe on the back of the head. Little Davie Betillo, a self-described "cabaret owner" who was willing to talk more than most, swore it was all done under direct orders from Lucky. According to Betillo, if the women stepped out of line, Luciano had some advice: "You gotta sit on them first, then step on them!"

When word trickled out that he was accused of being a pimp, Lucky was little more than annoyed. He considered the prostitution racket to be "worse than dope" and figured no one would believe such a trumped-up charge. It was common knowledge that he had washed his hands of such activity, although if some of his men wanted to make a little money on the side, that was their business. His irritation grew when he found out that witnesses were being promised immunity in exchange for testifying against him. He had some of his men stake out the building where the girls were being questioned, but to no avail. It was impossible to get at them to persuade them to recant. When they weren't spilling their guts in Dewey's office, they were closely guarded by his agents. Still, Lucky convinced himself that nothing would come of the investigation. He refused to believe that these small-time criminals could take down a major player like himself.

In March of 1936, as he paced the floor worrying about these developments, Lucky received a disturbing phone call from the building manager. Some men, official-looking types, were making their way upstairs to his apartment. They had specifically asked not to be announced. The blood drained from Lucky's face as he assessed the situation. The unthinkable was happening. Certain that they were police officers carrying a warrant for his arrest, Lucky crammed all the money he had into his pockets and escaped down the service elevator to freedom.

The Great Escape

Though later he would quip that it was "a good time to take a vacation," Lucky's next moves speak more of panic than planning. From New York, he made his way to Philadelphia, where he traded in his car for fresh wheels and, ever the dandy, bought himself an entire new wardrobe. From there he journeyed to Cleveland, where he hopped a southbound train. The fugitive's final destination was, of all places, a well-known spa town just outside of Little Rock, Arkansas.

It was quite a journey for a man who liked to conduct his business from the comfort of his living room couch. Hot Springs, however, was no ordinary resort. At the time, the town's two casinos were run by a shady character named

Owney Madden, nicknamed "the Killer" thanks to a longtime hobby of his. Under his considerable financial influence, the place had become a refuge for mobsters on the lam. There they could evade the long arm of the law, indulge in a little gambling, and relax in the healing waters that gave the vacation spot its name. This haven was also sheltered by what were, even by the standards of the time, astonishingly corrupt forces of law and order. Lucky spent his time of exile in exceptional comfort, and even summoned his current mistress, Russian showgirl Gay Orlova, to keep him company — all the while under the solicitous eye of the local police.

Meanwhile, back in New York, after learning of Lucky's abrupt departure, Dewey and his men scrambled to regain control of the situation. On April 1, Dewey publicly proclaimed Charles "Lucky" Luciano Public Enemy Number One and warned that Lucky would be arrested on sight. When it leaked out that Lucky was in fact taking a pleasant vacation in the southern state, accompanied by his glamorous girlfriend, Dewey immediately ordered his arrest and extradition. The local sheriff was obliged to act. With effusive apologies, he reluctantly snapped the cuffs on his northern visitor.

The local Mob-controlled courts set bail at $5000, pocket change for a man of Lucky's stature. But his freedom was short-lived. Dewey complained so loudly about this travesty of justice that the fugitive was quickly rearrested, this time by order of the governor of Arkansas. While in custody, the pampering continued. The Mob boss was given free rein of the sheriff's office. He sat at the lawman's desk making long-distance calls on the office phone while his girlfriend perched seductively on his knee. It was business as usual for Lucky, even after his arrest.

One of those phone calls was to summon his pricey New York lawyer to his side. Determined to protect Lucky against the 90 counts of compulsory prostitution that were being brought against him, he drafted a statement in Lucky's name in an attempt to clear his client. Complaining he was the victim of "the most vicious kind of politics," Lucky asserted his innocence, saying he would never stoop to anything as vulgar as prostitution. "I have never been involved in anything so messy," he told the press. He wisely stopped short of proclaiming himself innocent of any other wrongdoing.

But it wasn't his lawyer who was offering him the best protection at this point. In a bizarre turn of events, the sheriff barricaded himself and his prisoner in the sanctuary of the jailhouse and refused to come out. He refused to hand over his guest to the Arkansas Rangers when they turned up to escort the accused to his hearing in the state capitol, for fear that they might mistreat him. Only when the Rangers threatened to storm the place and take him by force did the sheriff relent. Lucky was dragged in chains to a cell in the nearby city, where 20 machine-gun-toting Rangers prevented his escape.

The state, eager to rid itself of its troublesome visitor, granted the order of extradition, despite the $25,000 bribe being offered to the attorney general to put an end to the proceedings. Lucky had the last word as he was being taken away. "I am being kidnapped," he allegedly groaned as police dragged him back to New York and the grand jury that awaited him.

Chapter 4
Gangster, Convict ... War Hero

A strategy meeting between Lucky Luciano, his lawyers, and his most trusted associates was taking place in Lucky's New York apartment, and it was not going in a direction that pleased him. Lucky could barely conceal his rage. Despite the multitude of crimes he had committed in the intervening years, this would be his first court date since he had been caught smuggling dope as a teenager. Lucky wanted assurances that his lawyers could win, that his men could bribe or force a positive outcome to the trial. He wasn't getting them.

Though the counts against him had dropped significantly, from 90 to 62, there were still signs that the prosecution meant to play hardball. Bail had been set at $350,000, an astronomical sum for the time. Even the multimillionaire gangster winced as he reached for his checkbook.

Lucky regretted running away in the first place. The press was painting him as a "whoremaster," he spat out. He should have let his lawyers handle the whole thing from the beginning. He turned to them now. "Do you mean to tell me Dewey expects to put me away because some crummy two-dollar whore says I was her boss?" he demanded explosively. The attorneys, the finest that money could buy, looked at each other and shrugged. His Mob advisors, the men he'd once called the best in the world, jumped in to reassure him. Any money they could scrounge up would be at his disposal, they pledged. Anything he needed done would also be done, they added significantly..

Their leader knew what they were referring to: the murder of his persecutor, Thomas Dewey. Lucky hesitated. Then, for the second time, he vetoed the idea. Despite the odds against him, he was still confident in his ability to come out on top.

The State v. Lucky Luciano

On May 13, 1936, the case of the State of New York v. Charles Luciano was brought to trial. Every day, Lucky slunk into the courthouse in lower Manhattan, the brim of his hat pulled down low to cover his face. Dozens of spectators turned up to gawk at the disgraced Mob boss. Dotted among them were plainclothes policemen, looking for signs of trouble. The man who had once flirted with celebrity now hid in shame as flashbulbs popped, cameras rolled, and newsmen shouted out his name.

Once seated before the judge, however, the Syndicate leader was forced to share the limelight. Beside him sat his codefendants in the case, all nine of them. Lucky was somewhat aghast at the company he was keeping. There was Jack Ellestein, James Federico, Jesse Jacobs, Meyer Berkman, and Little Davie Betillo, the one man with acknowledged ties to the Mob boss. Benny Spiller, Abe Wahnman, Thomas Pennochio, and Ralph "the Pimp" Liguori rounded out the group. Four others had decided to plead guilty and turn state's evidence. These were small-time hoods whose names would be long forgotten had they not been Lucky's co-accused in this vice trial.

Dewey went straight for the jugular. Together, the defendants controlled more than 200 brothels throughout the city, he claimed, and had forced over 3000 women to work in these dens of iniquity, netting a whopping $12 million a year. Witness after witness backed him up, 68 of them in total. Most of these were "working girls" who plucked at the jury's heartstrings with tales of abuse and enslavement at the hands of the parasites seated before them. They had arrived in the big city as naive young girls, they claimed as one, only to be forced into prostitution by vicious pimps who would beat them and drug them to keep them compliant. Each girl was quick to add that, while under the prosecutor's care, her drug addiction had been miraculously cured.

Most damning was the tale told by a woman named Nancy Presser. Nancy claimed to have once been a high-class escort whose services could be purchased for the princely sum of $100 a night. Drugs, misery, and the ravages of time had reduced her to a shell of a woman who sold her favors for two or three dollars a shot. Unable to withstand the vicious beatings her pimp doled out, she had turned to Lucky Luciano for help. She said that, at her lowest, he had sheltered her in his luxury home, which she was able to describe in detail. He had also helped her out financially, giving her hundreds of dollars out of his own pocket until she could get back on her feet.

While under his care, she continued, she had often overheard phone conversations between Lucky and his cronies, outlining details of the vice ring they ran. When Dewey asked if she had to trade sexual favors for the crime lord's care, she denied it. "Charlie couldn't," she explained. "You know what I mean?" There was a gasp from the packed courthouse, and the accused nearly leapt out of his seat. His lawyer, George Levy, grabbed him by the sleeve of his conservative gray suit and hauled him back into his chair. For good measure, he ground his heel into his client's foot as a reminder to behave. It's likely this was the first time anyone had dared to manhandle Lucky Luciano and lived to tell the tale.

Under cross-examination, Nancy Presser faltered, like many of the witnesses. She confessed that she couldn't recall the exact location of the apartment building where she and

Lucky had supposedly had their little tryst. And she admitted that "perhaps" the prosecution might have shown her photographs of the interior to refresh her memory prior to testifying. Her testimony, like that of the other women, seemed either fabricated or a vindictive exaggeration.

Regardless of the questionable reliability of these witnesses, Lucky Luciano was acting like a guilty man. Red-faced and sweating, he could barely conceal his agitation. It wasn't so much the obvious lies the women were telling that disconcerted him. It was the one little detail they all kept referring to that got under his skin. Lucky was impotent, they said repeatedly. The attack on his manhood, though embarrassing, was likely true. He would freely admit, after all, that his recurring bouts of syphilis and gonorrhea as a teen had excluded him from fighting in the First World War. They had probably had other more lasting effects as well. The suggestion of impotency stung him more than any of the other accusations leveled against him.

The biggest boost to the prosecution's case probably came from Lucky himself. Once on the stand, he leaned back in his chair and tried to project the image of a man confident of his own innocence. The jury received a different impression than the one he wished to convey. The *capo* contradicted himself frequently and told bald-faced lies when the truth would have served him better. He also blurted out self-incriminating truths when he should have denied everything. His lawyers must have winced throughout his performance.

His greatest misstep came when he strenuously denied knowing any of the witnesses, then promptly backtracked. As a dashing man about town, he said, he was often in the company of some unsavory characters, perhaps even his codefendants. And as a bachelor, he wasn't above paying for female companionship. It was entirely possible, he conceded, that he had come into contact with many, if not all, of the witnesses. Thomas Dewey looked on in triumph. These words were tantamount to admitting his guilt.

Lucky was equally at a loss when the subject of his finances was brought up. "My business is gambling houses and booking horses," he stated, earning the laughter of the crowd when he made reference to his modest financial status. Anyone who had seen his ravishing girlfriend, Gay Orlova, in a recent press conference knew better. The unemployed showgirl had turned up, dripping in diamonds and furs, claiming that it was out of character for her beau to do something that wasn't "nice," such as running prostitutes. Lucky's notoriety was working against him. As a witness, he was proving to be his own worst enemy.

Dewey made every effort to paint the accused in a sinister light. In a dramatic gesture, he jumped to his feet and accused Lucky of witness tampering. Many of the prostitutes had recently been approached by menacing strangers, he cried, who had threatened to exterminate them if they testified. "Have you gentlemen," he demanded of the jury, "ever known stark, complete, and paralyzing terror?" The courtroom rang with shocked gasps and exclamations. The horrified judge slammed down his gavel and immediately issued a bench warrant seeking the arrest of those responsible. Though he mentioned no name, all eyes turned towards the prime defendant. Things were looking darker and darker for the Mafia boss.

On Sunday, June 7, the jury announced that they had reached a verdict. The accused braced themselves as each of the 62 counts was read out. Like clockwork, the response in each case was "guilty." The most lenient sentence the judge imposed for one of the minor players was two to four years; the harshest was reserved for the alleged kingpin, the "greatest gangster in America" as Dewey called him, who drew 30 to 50 years, an unheard-of sentence for the crime of compulsory prostitution. He was dragged from the courtroom, still insisting he was innocent. Perhaps he even believed it. No one was more stunned at the outcome of the trial than Lucky Luciano himself.

In a press conference soon after the trial, Dewey freely admitted that the case was a sham. "This, of course, was not a vice trial," he stated. "It was a racket prosecution." The admission was a hollow victory for Lucky as he was hauled off in shackles to prison.

Lucky in Siberia

Located in Upper New York State, Dannemora State Penitentiary had long been known as "Siberia" for its remote location and the icy winds that cut through its thick stone walls. Fidgeting on his rock-hard cot in the middle of his bone-chilling cell, Lucky tried to keep busy as he awaited the results of his appeal. He instructed his brother Bart to put his possessions in storage, and made sure his girlfriend was taken care of financially in his absence. He appointed his old friend Frank Costello to be his representative on the outside. There was little else to occupy him in the meantime.

Only a few months earlier, Lucky had been on top of the world. A beautiful home, expensive clothes, an adoring girlfriend, men obeying his every command — all of it had been his. Now his fine wardrobe was in mothballs and he was forced to wear drab prison garb, his inmate number, 92168, stitched on his chest. His expensive haircut was butchered by the jailhouse barber. What was worse, a prison supervisor had deemed him a drug addict and recommended constant supervision. He was confined to his cell for all but a few hours a day. His freedom was truly gone. Lucky called his new dwelling a "sewer" and grumbled that the harsh rules he was forced to obey were "un-American."

This was not the ideal time for the crime lord to be behind bars. Over the past couple of years, his top advisors, the men he had been running with since he was just another street punk, had slowly started to drift away. Meyer Lansky was often in Cuba, which he dreamed of transforming into a gambling mecca. Dashing Bugsy Siegel was off schmoozing with celebrities in Hollywood. Vito Genovese, under scrutiny by the law, had recently received permission from the Unione Siciliane to escape across the ocean to Italy. Others, terrified by the imprisonment of their previously infallible boss, were scrambling to protect themselves and their operations. Though his men promised to stand by him through thick and thin, Lucky was unsure how to keep his empire intact while he was in prison. His only chance lay in his appeal.

Lucky's lawyers believed that the key to winning lay in getting witnesses to recant their testimony. Unfortunately, many of the prostitutes had been given all-expenses-paid trips to Europe immediately after the trial, courtesy of the prosecution. With the key witnesses out of the country, the lawyers' hands were tied. Lucky's appeal was denied. He would spend the next few decades behind bars. His first chance to seek parole wouldn't be until 1956. In the meantime, he would be just another jailbird.

To his men, though, Lucky was still *capo*. They continued to seek him out, pestering him for instruction and counsel. He did what he could, but it was a little hard to conduct business when armed guards stood a stone's throw away.

For the next six years, Lucky bent over backwards to fashion a comfortable life for himself. He quickly discovered that bribery worked just as well on the inside as it did on the outside. Assigned laundry duty (in the era before electric washing machines were widely available), he quickly bought his way out of that unpleasant chore. A few dollars here and there bought him safety from the more hardened criminals, some of whom he attempted to recruit to his organization. With time on his hands, he worked to better himself, poring over history books from the prison library and practicing his penmanship in the evenings by lamplight. To cheer himself up when he felt down, he listened to the comedy routines of Abbott & Costello on the radio.

Occasionally, a family member turned up to visit him, but seeing them upset him terribly. After one such visit, he was so frustrated and ashamed that he smashed his head repeatedly against the wall of his cell, injuring himself so badly he required stitches. Life might have continued in this way until he was old and gray, but for an event that would change the world: the outbreak of World War II.

Lucky the War Hero

Lucky Luciano was one of the few people who was relieved when the war started. "All that crap," as he put it, kept his name out of the papers, after all. He was also fascinated by newspaper reports of warfare in Europe, and he even half-seriously threatened to put a hit on Adolf Hitler. The war had a more direct effect on him, too. The prostitutes who had been witnesses in his trial began to drift back from overseas. Lucky's lawyers tracked them down and begged them to sign affidavits stating that Dewey had instructed them to lie on the stand. Many of the women did so, including the prosecution's star witness, Nancy Presser. This was bad news for the prosecutor, who was preparing to run for governor and would eventually make two bids for the presidency, in 1944 and 1948. The crime boss could make things very unpleasant for him if he wished.

Another event bolstered Lucky's hopes for freedom. One day, out of the blue, the warden summoned him to his office, where a man was waiting to meet him. The stranger said his name was Haffender and explained that he was there as a representative of the navy. "Wet behind the ears," was Lucky's initial impression of the man. Perhaps, Haffender said, Lucky had heard of the recent tragic events concerning the S.S. *Normandie*. Lucky nodded. News of the sinking of the famed battleship in February 1942, right in the middle of the Brooklyn Navy Yard, had been splashed across the front page of all the papers. The entire country had responded with fear and outrage. But Lucky couldn't understand what this had to do with him.

Haffender explained. The government had become concerned about the safety of its naval fleet on home turf. In fact, it was desperate. What it needed was someone with influence over the longshoremen who worked the New York docks, someone who could direct them to protect the ships against further sabotage. Many of these men were of Italian heritage; they would respect the orders of one of their own. The navy, Haffender explained to the incredulous convict, thought he was the man for the job. And in return, he added, they would do their utmost to help him out of his current situation.

Lucky knew it would be futile to ask for parole. Instead, he requested a change of venue, somewhere more comfortable where he could have better access to the outside world. His request was granted. Within days, he was transferred to the Great Meadows Prison, a "country club" facility where he was permitted a certain amount of freedom. He was provided with good meals, fine wines, comfortable quarters, and office facilities. He was even permitted to take day trips to nearby Albany. There, he could wander at will under the watchful eye of a chaperone. One glorious evening, he was allowed to meet his girlfriend, Gay, at a restaurant. The two feasted on a steak dinner before retiring to a private room. It was his first taste of freedom in years.

More importantly, Lucky was now permitted to communicate freely with the men in his organization. Albert Anastasia, he knew, had strong ties with the longshoremen of New York, including his brother, a dock worker known as "Tough Tony." He would contact him, he told Haffender, and see what transpired.

Though the exact details of what transpired between the longshoremen and Lucky's middleman were kept under wraps, it was clear the navy thought his efforts were successful. There were no further acts of sabotage along the docks and "Operation Underworld," as the navy dubbed it, was deemed a triumph.

Lucky's stay at Great Meadows was extended indefinitely. Shortly thereafter, he was approached by more military men. This time, he was given a tougher task. He was asked to use his Mafia ties to gather intelligence on the Axis forces in Italy, particularly in Sicily. Again, his actions were deemed a success. Lucky was moving ever closer to freedom.

There is a more cynical version of these events, however. Critics have suggested that Lucky's supposed war efforts were actually a con orchestrated by his dear friend, the sharp-witted Meyer Lansky. In an elaborate setup, Lansky, it's said, had encouraged Albert Anastasia to blow up the *Normandie* and commit similar acts of sabotage around the dockyards. He then dropped a few hints in the ears of certain influential friends, saying that the imprisoned Mob boss was the only man with the authority to put an end to the destruction. When the navy did contact Lucky in prison, Anastasia then received the order to stop the violence.

When his superior was not immediately paroled, the story goes, Lansky reminded those same influential friends that, as head of the American Mafia, Lucky likely had some valuable allies back in the old country. At his request, they would gladly act as his spies. Lucky, of course, actually despised the Sicilian Mafia, and the feeling was mutual. A decade before, he had murdered two of their American representatives, Masseria and Maranzano, in order to further his own career. Why would the Sicilians cooperate with someone who had assassinated two of their own?

The military, however, seemed convinced that Lucky had behaved honorably and fulfilled his part of the agreement.

The information he gave them was sound, they insisted; Haffender supplied them with a discreetly worded letter confirming Lucky's cooperation. The only group of people left to convince were the members of the parole board. On May 7, 1945, they received a petition from the Syndicate leader's lawyers. As well as being a model prisoner, Charles Luciano was a national hero, they were told. He was a reformed man who had used his time behind bars to render what they ambiguously termed "a definite service to the war effort." They had a letter of recommendation from Haffender to back up their claims. The petition was passed along to the new governor, none other than Thomas Dewey, who had ridden his status as a crime-busting celebrity to the state's top spot.

The man who had once gone after the crime lord like a pit bull was surprisingly favorable in his response. Perhaps he was impressed by the services Lucky claimed to have rendered to his country. It might also have been gratitude on Dewey's part. In 1940, a reporter had informed him that a contract had been put out on his life, and that Lucky had nixed the murder. But the most likely explanation was that Dewey was thinking of his reputation. If it was revealed that he had coerced witnesses in the alleged prostitution ring all those years ago, his career would be over.

Lucky, however, claimed that the leniency Dewey showed was motivated by something quite different: simple greed. Dewey was as crooked as every other politician he'd come across, Lucky crowed. The incorruptible paragon, he charged, was given $90,000 of dirty money to fund his political career. These accusations dogged the governor for the rest of his career — and likely cost him a shot at the presidency.

In February 1946, Lucky Luciano was finally granted parole. But it was a bittersweet victory for the *capo.* Despite his heroic conduct during the war, he was still considered a danger to his country. Once he passed through the prison gates, he was transported not to his luxury home in New York City, but to a place he'd last seen as a young boy. It was Ellis Island, where immigrants and exiles alike were held. As bureaucrats finalized the last of the paperwork, Lucky paced his small, impersonal room. In a matter of hours, he would board the S.S. *Laura Keene.* Its destination: the port town of Genoa, Italy. As a condition of his parole, Lucky had been banished from American soil for the rest of his life.

Chapter 5
Exile in Italy

When Lucky was first thrown in jail, a parole officer had made an eight-page assessment of the Mob leader's personality for the benefit of the court. Among his findings, he remarked on the Syndicate leader's astounding "attitude of nonchalance" in the face of danger, coupled with a "peasantlike faith in chance." These characteristics were certainly in evidence as Lucky prepared to mount the gangplank. Though he shed a few tears as he said his goodbyes to his brothers and sisters (his parents were long dead), he was a different man once he boarded the ship. As reporters milled around on the dock, craning to see what was going on, he eagerly joined in the raucous party that was in full swing on board.

In attendance was the cream of the criminal underworld.

Mingling with them were many top-ranking officials who were in deep with the Mob. Lucky claimed that the mayor of New York himself was there to see him off and enjoy a free lobster dinner.

While many of his old acquaintances were glad to see Lucky, many more were glad to see him go. Nevertheless, they boisterously toasted his health with goblets of champagne and loudly wished him "bon voyage."

In the midst of the chatter and laughter, a slight figure drew the guest of honor into a dark corner. Meyer Lansky had arrived with a going-away present for his old friend. He knew that years of paying out exorbitant lawyers' fees had drained his boss's bank account. Lucky had little left other than the suit on his back and the dusty furniture his brother had put in storage all those years ago. Meyer handed Lucky a smart leather suitcase, stuffed with as much as a million dollars, according to rumors. Lucky embraced him in gratitude. His friend had another surprise in store for him. In the cabin next to his were three pretty girls, his for the duration of the voyage.

A less welcome companion was Murray Weinstein, the New York detective who would ensure that Lucky made no unplanned detours on the voyage to Italy. Surprisingly, Lansky and Lucky had no such plan in mind. As always, the Mob boss decided to trust his good fortune. The two-week journey proved to be an uneventful one. Once on Italian shores, though, Lucky faced a less-than-welcoming reception. As soon as he stepped off the gangplank, he walked straight into the arms of the local police.

Starting Over in Italy

In a gray room in a grayer building, the American exile craned forward. Lucky's Italian was a little rusty but, as far as he could tell, the bureaucrats of his native country were debating whether they could send the troublesome gangster straight back to the U.S. After much discussion, they concluded that they couldn't legally take such an action. Though a naturalized citizen of the United States, Lucky had nonetheless been born on Italian soil. Like it or not, he was their problem now.

The officials decided to keep Lucky as far away as possible from the temptations a big city might offer. The best place for him, they decreed, was with his relatives, in the tiny mining town of Lercara Friddi on the island of Sicily. Lucky had only vague memories of his home town. When he last saw it, he'd been a boy of eight. But the townspeople certainly remembered him. Impoverished though they were, they greeted him like royalty. His reputation as a world-famous crook preceded him. In their eyes, he was a celebrity, and they were delighted he was among them once more.

Lucky walked around Lercara Friddi's town square in a daze the evening of his arrival. Fireworks sparkled in the night sky. Children ran underfoot, squealing. The wine flowed and the food was rich and plentiful. It was the kind of celebration usually reserved for high holidays. The whole town, it seemed, had come out to welcome him. Long-lost relatives clasped him in their arms. Even the mayor had turned up, beaming, to shake his hand.

Though he was grateful for the reception, the banished gangster knew he couldn't stay. The stench of sulfur from the mines filled his nostrils, tainted the wine, and coated his clothes with a fine yellow dust. It was as far from the bright lights of Broadway as could be imagined. This town even lacked a movie theater!

Within weeks, Lucky abandoned this warm, welcoming place for the bright lights of Rome, where he could live a little, set up some connections, and take advantage of his anonymity. As a criminal, Lucky was forced to relearn his craft from the bottom up. Once in the big city, he started out small, dabbling in the black market that had exploded into existence during Italy's post-war depression. Booze and cigarettes supplied by U.S. soldiers were the cornerstones of the underground economy. Lucky was self-conscious about his lowly status, though he never hooked up with the Sicilian Mafia in all the years he spent in Europe. A "private club," he called it, one he was never invited to join. While he was a bit player in Italy, he was still *capo di tutti capi* in his mind. "All that black market crap was just somethin' to keep my mind occupied," he insisted, not a way to keep his head above water.

In the fall of 1946, after months of twiddling his thumbs in cafes and anonymous hotels, Lucky received the signal he had been waiting for all along. An anonymous courier dropped off an envelope at the door to his hotel room. In it was a crisp white sheet of paper with a cryptic message. "December — Hotel Nacional," it read. Lucky could feel his excitement mounting. The plan had finally been set in motion.

Lucky suspected that, since he'd arrived in Italy, he had been watched by local police and perhaps even the CIA. Illegal drugs were a hot commodity in post-war Europe, and many believed the exiled kingpin of American crime was not above channeling cheap heroin back to the States. But Lucky had other plans. The mysterious note that was slipped into his hand was a summons from his *consigliere*, Lansky, notifying him of an underworld conference in Havana, Cuba. For months, they had been plotting his escape to the Caribbean island. The *capo* had secretly taken an Italian passport under his real name, Salvatore Lucania, and acquired visas under that name for Mexico and South America, as well as Cuba.

Gambling on Havana

The ruse was a success. "We breezed through customs and nobody looked at me twice," Lucky chuckled.

In high-rolling Havana, everything was for sale. The notorious gangster rented a fully staffed house by the seashore in one of the better residential areas and, before long, the city's elite were clamoring to meet him. He was finally free to indulge in his favorite pursuits: golfing, gambling, and chasing women. It reminded him of the golden era before his decade-long imprisonment. Lucky abandoned his stuffy suit and tie for shorts and sandals, ideal for lounging on the beach. For the first time in years, he felt relaxed and confident.

Despite his relaxed demeanor, he had a serious purpose: Cuba was to be his new center of operations, and he and Lansky had called an underworld conference to announce he was back on the scene.

Nestled in the conference room at the Hotel Nacional, Lucky reminisced about the old days. Four floors of the hotel/casino had been reserved for him and the boys. As always, business would mix with pleasure. But the entertainment wouldn't be provided by squealing showgirls this time. The "official" reason for the gathering was to honor someone whose fortunes had been closely tied to their own for many years: the Syndicate was throwing a bash to salute the world-famous crooner, Frank Sinatra. "A good kid," Lucky said warmly as the entertainer took the stage.

In a dubious show of solidarity, Old Blue Eyes even had his picture snapped with his arm slung around Lucky's shoulder, and he presented the don with a gold cigarette case. The inscription inside it read: "To my dear pal Lucky, from his friend, Frank." The singer was later to regret the show of intimacy. In the early 1950s, a petrified, chain-smoking Sinatra was brought before federal authorities who demanded to know why he had fraternized with well-known mobsters. In particular, they wanted to know what he had carried in his suitcase on that trip to Cuba — rumor had it that it contained two million, cash, for his "dear pal" Lucky. Sinatra denied the charge emphatically, however, saying the bag had merely contained the usual toiletries and, surprisingly, art supplies. His affection for Lucky just didn't stretch that far, he insisted. For him, the Havana conference was just another singing gig.

When the music and partying were done, the guest of honor was ushered out and the gangsters got down to business. Two men were conspicuous by their absence, however. Al Capone and Bugsy Siegel were nowhere to be seen. It would have been indiscreet to invite them, since it was known that neither was long for this world: Scarface Al was dying from the syphilis that was eating away at his sanity, and Bugs would soon take a bullet through the eye courtesy of a Murder, Inc. gunman.

The Siegel situation was one of the hot topics at the conference. It had been discovered that the Mob's charming friend had been pilfering from its coffers to fund his glamorous lifestyle of stretch limos and Hollywood starlets. Even Meyer Lansky, his childhood companion, regretfully agreed to the motion to eliminate him. "Benny's got to be hit," he said with a great show of sorrow. When Lucky, equally regretful, put his seal on it, the hit was a done deal. Business, as always, took precedence over personal feelings.

At the last conference in Chicago, Lucky had made a point of refusing both the tribute money and the title of boss of bosses. This time, he graciously accepted both honors. The money, amounting to tens of thousands of dollars, would be invested in the Hotel Nacional. The elegant casino in its picturesque setting was a sure-fire money-maker, he thought gleefully. The title of boss, he reasoned, would quickly reestablish his dominance after years of exile and imprisonment.

Havana was less than 100 miles from U.S. soil, Lucky reminded the assembled mobsters, and would make an ideal headquarters for the organization. He would be close enough to keep an eye on things, yet just out of reach of the American authorities. Lucky decided it would be too upsetting to mention that he had been toying with the notion of marrying a Cuban girl — any Cuban girl — and giving up his American citizenship to take on a Cuban passport. For now, he would let his men enjoy the beach, the parties, and the gambling. He would break the news to them gently, at a later date.

Then he broached the real reason behind the summit. Mafia infighting had reached fever pitch. Mobsters were battling over power and territory as they had in the old days, before establishing the Unione Siciliane. Their leader warned them to make peace. They all had the same ambition, he pointed out, which was, as always, to make themselves as rich as kings.

Once the sound of applause faded away, Lucky was left with a troubled feeling. Something had changed. When he looked out at the assembled mobsters, he saw more wrinkles and more gray hairs, but there was another, subtler difference as well. The polite response had been tinged with an emotion he couldn't quite put his finger on — resentment, maybe. Though he had been in constant contact with his underlings over the years, many of them had grown too self-reliant and ambitious. One man in particular could barely conceal the sneer of contempt on his face.

Since fleeing a murder rap in New York in 1937, Vito Genovese's career had taken some unusual turns. During his self-imposed exile in Italy, he had cozied up to the ruthless Benito Mussolini and had been chief drug dealer to the dictator's cocaine-addicted son-in-law. After the war, he had remained in Italy, serving as an interpreter and spy for the U.S. Army, only to use his connections to corner the black market. He had returned to the States only when the last witness in his murder case had been strategically murdered.

Since then, Lucky learned, he had moved into drug dealing on a large scale and had earned a reputation as a troublemaker among his Unione brothers. He attempted to muscle in on other men's turf and tried to provoke the Unione into putting a contract out on an outsider, a top narcotics agent who was hounding him. To add insult to injury, Genovese was dropping hints that he thought Lucky should retire, no doubt hoping the top spot would then become his.

Lucky, of course, had no intention of retiring, and he told Genovese as much in a private meeting in his hotel room. He scolded his former lieutenant, telling him to curb his drug-dealing activities — they were drawing too much negative attention to the outfit. Genovese, of course, refused to listen and suggested, in very impolite terms, that his superior was both out of touch and washed up. Before long, voices were raised and the first blows were being traded. It was a clear violation of the "no hands rule" that forbade members of the Unione from assaulting one another, on penalty of death. But Lucky was in an unstoppable fury. He vented his pent-up rage on the other man, knocking him to the ground and pounding him with his fists.

Always calculating, Lucky was careful not to hit his opponent in the face. Any visible sign of damage would be legitimate cause for the other to press for a hit on him. When the vicious beating was over, Genovese lay gasping where he fell. He suffered three broken ribs and a fractured arm. Lucky, nursing his bruised knuckles, threatened to shoot Genovese between the eyes if he squealed. The Mob boss then announced to the other conference-goers that Genovese had retired to his room after a sudden attack of the flu. It took the unfortunate gangster three days of bed rest to recover from his injuries.

After the conference broke up, the Syndicate leader retreated to his plush, antique-filled mansion. He was a worried man. Though he had won the fight, the incident with Genovese was a clear sign his power was waning. The feud, he knew, was just beginning, and Genovese was the type who liked to solve his problems with a bullet. It would take both brains and brawn to outmaneuver him.

To console himself, Lucky began running around with

a pretty young socialite who was smitten with his tough-guy image. Though he had meant to keep a low profile in his new home, he was seen with his new conquest sunning on the beach, rolling dice at the casino, and nuzzling at parties. The Cuban papers, of course, were quick to publish candid photos of the two lovebirds. It soon leaked out that the Salvatore Lucania who was gracing the society pages was none other than the notorious crime lord, Lucky Luciano. Before long, the U.S. government was aware of it, too.

In February 1947, Lucky found himself once again in police custody. Never one to turn down a photo op, he cheerfully agreed to pose for the cameras with the arresting officers. The prison camp, located in the middle of a swamp, was a far cry from the plush accommodations he had become used to, however. Lucky wrestled with heat, sweat, and mosquitoes while his lawyers wrestled with immigration authorities. But the negotiations were doomed from the start. The U.S., which still had trade relations with the pre-revolutionary country, placed an embargo on medical supplies until Cuba agreed to turn Lucky over.

Lansky and Lucky's dream of running their empire from Havana was a dismal failure. In the spring, to very little fanfare, the crime lord was flung, much like other cargo, onto a battered Turkish freighter and sent on his way back to Italy.

Caught in a Web of Red Tape

After the grueling, month-long journey, the exhausted

traveler found himself in a familiar spot: the grim interior of a foreign prison. Lucky's Cuban escapade had been a public embarrassment to Italian policy-makers. The Unione leader was considered a threat to national security, and a commission was formed to determine his fate. The commission suggested that he be confined for five years to Lercara Friddi, under the care of his relatives. Lucky was aghast at the idea. Even five minutes in that backwater town was too much. He swore right and left that he had merely been vacationing in Cuba. "I never intended to abandon my Italian citizenship," he lied.

After weeks of debate, a ruling was made in his favor. He could move freely about Italy but was forbidden to leave the country without permission. As a final, futile warning, he was instructed to "abstain from any illicit activity." Lucky agreed to the terms and was released from custody. This was just the beginning of his entanglement with Italian bureaucracy.

By summer, Lucky was back in Rome, dabbling once more in the black market, but it wasn't long before he was behind bars again. When news of Bugsy Siegel's murder reached Italy, Lucky was arrested on suspicion of orchestrating the overseas hit. Lucky, of course, denied all knowledge of the crime, which was true in a way. He knew little of the details. "All they hadda tell me was the results," he grumbled.

As usual, he was released due to lack of evidence, after nine days of incarceration. Though he was a free man once more, he seemed strangely jumpy, as if he was being hunted.

Lucky decided that he had gone without protection long enough. It was time to beef up security. Because living out of a hotel room made him vulnerable, he demanded that every key to his room be handed over to him. From now on, no one, from the scrubwoman to the hotel manager, would be permitted to enter his domain without supervision. Couriers were forbidden to come near him — all mail was to be presented to the front desk.

At that point, Lucky was receiving tens of thousands of dollars per month from his overseas interests, money that was hand-delivered by Mafia runners. However, he was clearly less worried about theft than he was about being caught alone by someone who could be doubling as an assassin. Eventually, his paranoia reached such a pitch that two husky bodyguards were hired to shadow him.

Lucky was clearly trying to ward off a Mob hit. Genovese, he was certain, meant to strike sometime soon. But law enforcement agents were also tailing him, waiting for him to slip up. They soon got their wish.

In Rome, the lonely Mob boss often socialized with other American expatriates, some of whom were very disreputable characters. Among these was Ralph Liguori, aka "The Pimp," one of his codefendants in the vice trial of a decade before.

In Italy, Liguori had branched out into an equally sordid business: dealing cocaine. Lucky, eager for contact with a fellow American, had unwisely let himself be spotted in the novice dealer's company. When Liguori was collared in a major drug bust, the cuffs were snapped on Lucky as well. While the case collapsed due to lack of evidence, the Syndicate leader was still punished. His passport was confiscated, a nightly curfew was imposed, and he was banished once more to Sicily. Lucky was convinced he'd been framed. Not by the police, or by the desperate Liguori, but by his enemy, Vito Genovese.

There was one bright spot in this period of turbulence and paranoia, and her name was Igea Lissoni. Igea was a lithe, blond dancer in her mid-20s. Her 50-year-old suitor started licking his chops the moment he laid eyes on her. Unlike most of his conquests, Igea was initially horrified by his attention. When he sent her gifts of flowers and perfume, she tossed them in the garbage. When he showed up at the nightclub to watch her dance, she hid backstage until he left. He was exactly the type of man her mother had warned her about when she left for the big city to make her fortune.

Lucky hadn't reached the top of his profession by intelligence and good planning alone. He was also known for his pleasant, ingratiating manner, which could charm anyone, from jaded police chiefs to innocent, religious young women. Eventually, Igea succumbed. She fell in love with the man she called "my Charlie." The only thing that stood between them was her proper, middle-class values. Before she would move in with him, she insisted on seeing a wedding ring on her finger. The confirmed bachelor agreed to the ring, but not to the wedding. She accompanied him on his banishment to Sicily, a bride in her mind only.

A Sweet Deal Turns Sour

Though Lucky would never quite do the honorable thing and marry Igea, he was willing to make other concessions to his new love. She persuaded him to stop living out of suitcases and settle down in a real home with her. Nervous about his criminal associations, she also convinced him to take on a legitimate business venture. A relative of his from Lercara Friddi presented him with the perfect opportunity to go straight.

The mobster invited his cousin to sit down with him over a cup of coffee and tell him about the enterprise. He and a friend had just launched a candy factory, his cousin explained. The bonbons were so succulent, so delicious, they were sure to be a hit. He offered a sugary sample to his famous relative. Lucky, who had a sweet tooth, nearly swooned over the confection. He agreed that the factory would surely be a success, as his cousin predicted. But where exactly did *he* come in? His cousin smiled and leaned in closer. Everything was set up and ready to go, he explained. All they needed was a few thousand lire to start with, and they were set for life. Lucky asked for a few days to think it over.

The offer was tempting in many ways. Still, ever since Lucky had arrived in Italy, people had been hounding him for handouts. Sometimes, he thought, his notoriety was a terrible burden. People believed he was made of money, but times were tough all over. Italy still hadn't recovered from the turmoil of the war. Everywhere he turned, there was a child tugging at his sleeve, begging for a stick of gum or a few coins. Relatives he had never heard of showed up at his door, pleading for his help. Shady characters approached him as he sat in the trattoria, offering the perfect investment opportunity. The minute he showed interest and looked into their affairs, however, they vanished. Unlike them, his cousin, his closest relative in Italy, was sure to be sound. Lucky thought of how proud Igea would be and handed over the cash.

Several months and $60,000 later, with not a cent of profit in his pocket, Lucky knew something was up. He stormed into his cousin's factory, demanding to know what had happened to his investment. His cousin fell to his knees and begged for mercy. The factory had, in fact, made money, but the profits had been embezzled by the cousin and an associate. There was nothing left for Lucky. Back home, such an action would have had a bloody outcome. But in Sicily, it was different. The man was family, so Lucky's hands were tied.

In a rage, Lucky demanded that control of the company be handed over to him. But it was too late. His cousin had bled the place dry. Lucky abandoned the venture but soon indulged his sweet tooth again, this time by pouring his money into a pastry shop. After two years, it went under as well. The gangster was flooded with a sentiment he hadn't felt in years: shame. Long ago, he had boasted of his business prowess. The president of General Motors had nothing on him, he had crowed. Now, some simple-minded peasants had conned him out of thousands of dollars, money he could ill afford to lose. What was worse, he had failed his beloved Igea. His attempts to go straight were a bust.

No matter which way he turned, Lucky was accused of wrongdoing. The drug rumors swirling around him were becoming increasingly intense. During his sojourn in Cuba, U.S. agents claimed drug smuggling had skyrocketed from that destination. Since his arrival in Europe, Italy had become known as a major conduit for narcotics. Rumors had even centered around his dealings with the candy factory — an entire shipment had been ruined when the innocuous boxes of sweets had been torn to pieces by over-zealous police officers. The Mob boss had had enough. "If I'm guilty of all I been accused of," he fumed, "why don't the Italian police arrest me and put me in jail?"

It wasn't for want of trying. Lucky was the subject of several failed sting operations. In one, a glamorous Italian "contessa" lured the Mob boss to her hotel room and, after dazzling him with her jewels, attempted to score some hard drugs from him. It was such an obvious setup that Lucky walked out on her, laughing.

From overseas came a more serious threat. An agent of the U.S. government, Charles Siragusa, was assigned to go deep undercover, posing as a drug baron. Unfortunately, his assignment was so hush-hush that the local police were never informed of his real identity. Only weeks after he arrived in town they arrested him, thrilled to get their hands on a big wheel in the narcotics trade.

Once free, Siragusa gave his superiors the rather feeble assurance that Lucky had "been in touch with the most notorious delinquents of the United States." He was unable, however, to find a single hint that his quarry was actually dealing heroin. The only sign of wrongdoing he uncovered was the Syndicate leader's failure to register his new Buick, a gift from Meyer Lansky. Lucky coughed up the fine and that was the end of Siragusa's persecution.

The constant harassment from the police was beginning to wear Lucky down. The press, too, wouldn't leave him alone. Though semi-retired from crime, he was more famous now than ever before. While he enjoyed the attention, he was displeased by the accusations leveled against him. "They are defaming me," he complained of the media, "and spoiling my reputation." One exceptionally persistent paparazzo was punched in the face by Lucky when he had the nerve to trail the *capo* to the door of his and Igea's apartment. Though his legend was growing, Lucky knew the truth. He was no longer the infallible leader whose every venture turned to gold. His business dealings were in tatters. He had lost his magic touch.

Chapter 6 American Homecoming

By the late 1950s, Lucky Luciano had emerged as a full-fledged icon on the streets of Italy, as oft-photographed as any of the marble statuary or ancient frescoes. At his home away from home, the racetrack, beaming tourists would gather around him, autograph books in hand. They hounded him at the sidewalk cafes and eateries where he was a fixture, begging for a moment of the great man's time.

Not far behind the tourists were the journalists from overseas, looking to fulfill the public's hunger for news of the reputed boss of bosses. Lucky frequently permitted himself to be photographed grinning broadly and holding a wine glass aloft, a tip of the hat to his bootlegging days. A decade and a half after his banishment, he was eager to play along with the press and was still considered "good copy" in the U.S., so much so that he hired a service to track his voluminous press clippings.

Those who met with him, however, were startled by a sudden change in Lucky's appearance. At 60, with his lined face and graying hair, the tired, bespectacled man was a far cry from the vibrant figure of days gone by. A bad back was supported by a brace and he often turned to health spas to recuperate from the pain.

But it wasn't the years of unending police harassment that were turning Lucky into a prematurely old man. In fact, the constant surveillance had ceased; "Luciano is behaving himself" was now the official word. Instead, Lucky had a more pressing concern: his ever-worsening financial situation.

Though the press still worshipped him as the king of crime, the aging mobster was having difficulty convincing his American counterparts that his word was still law. The couriers still appeared at his door each month, but the cash-stuffed envelopes were looking more and more meager each time they met. Still reeling from his business failures, Lucky was chagrined. Two more of his business ventures — an electrical appliance store and a shop selling medical equipment — had both gone under. As a humble shopkeeper, the "king of crime" had proven to be a resounding failure.

There were other drains on Lucky's bank account as well. The lifelong gambler had bought himself a racehorse, another sure-fire money-maker, he thought with delight.

But Lucky's luck was running out. The horse was a dud, his investment a failure. It was whispered that he had lost tens of thousands on the transaction.

Along with his business failures, Lucky's many personal expenses were also a drain on his finances. He was as determined as ever to live in the lap of luxury. His home, with its gleaming marble floors and elegant floral decor, was an impressive sight to behold. In addition to the cost of maintaining such a luxurious home and lifestyle, there were always distant cousins ringing the doorbell, begging for a handout from their rich, famous relative. Poor men had no such "cousins," Lucky moaned as he reached for his wallet. But, desperate to keep up appearances, he could never turn them away empty-handed.

At times it seemed like his generosity might be his undoing. Lucky became known as a soft touch, and not only to family members. Any stranger with a sob story could walk away hundreds, even thousands of dollars richer. He was notorious for giving freely to charities as well. Though he was raised Catholic and hung an image of the Madonna and child in his bedroom, he was hardly a church-going man. But when a priest approached him, looking to raise funds to build a 120-bed hospital in the countryside to benefit the local peasantry, Lucky felt obliged to contribute. He gave what he could, but with money so tight he suggested to Father Scarpato an alternative method of raising funds.

Together, the two cooked up an ingenious scheme.

The gangster would import slot machines into the country, and the priest would distribute them and use the proceeds to build his clinic. Though it was a move of hazy morality and dubious legality, the two unlikely allies reasoned that it wasn't so very different from church-run bingo games.

The machines found their way into shops and nightspots throughout Italy, and the construction of the hospital was underway. Before long, though, the police got wind of this little arrangement. Unlicensed slot machines, even ones benefiting such a noble cause, were prohibited by law. Work was immediately and permanently halted on the hospital project and Father Scarpato was thrown into jail, his dreams shattered and his reputation in ruins. Lucky, though he professed to be horrified by the outcome of his actions, was never brought to justice for his involvement in the scam.

While corrupting a priest was a very serious matter, it was not at the forefront of Lucky's thoughts. He was following the fortunes of his Unione brothers with increasing despair. Joe Adonis, also an exile in Italy, was leading what seemed to be a life of suspicious luxury. To Lucky, it was more proof that he was being cut out of the Unione's profits while others grew fat on the fruits of his labor. There was little he could do about it. He retaliated rather feebly by refusing to communicate any longer with his one-time bootlegging partner. "I got nothin' in common with types like him," he sneered.

More alarming still was the violence being perpetrated against some of his top men. Frank Costello had recently announced his desire for retirement, complete with pension. The break with tradition nearly cost Costello his life when an assassin's bullet came within inches of penetrating his skull.

Albert Anastasia wasn't as fortunate. Lucky had considered Anastasia the last of his real allies, but Anastasia's loyalty was his downfall. He met his bloody end in 1957, in a hail of bullets in the middle of a New York barbershop. As leader of the Syndicate, Lucky should have been the one to veto or approve such drastic actions, but he had been kept out of the decision-making process. He suspected that the man he referred to as "the genius," Meyer Lansky, was withholding both funds and information in an effort to usurp Lucky's position. He no longer considered Lansky an ally, let alone a friend.

But his former friend's betrayal, while infuriating, was nothing compared to the actions of the man he considered his greatest enemy: Vito Genovese. Lucky's paranoia regarding his one-time lieutenant had reached the breaking point. He was certain he was next on Genovese's hit list. As a result, he wouldn't step into his car without first having it searched for evidence of sabotage.

But the attack, when it came, wasn't a bomb, as Lucky feared it would be. In June of 1957, as he stood waiting in his garage while his bodyguards examined his car for signs of tampering, he was startled by the sound of footsteps echoing on the concrete floor behind him. Sensing something was amiss, he spun around on his heels and confronted two men bearing down on him with their arms upraised. In their hands they clutched not pistols, but lethal-looking lead pipes. Lucky jumped out of their path as the pipes smashed downwards, harmlessly bouncing off the fender of his car. With a howl of rage, Lucky and his two bodyguards sprang on the would-be hit men and beat them into submission.

When the assault was over, the perpetrators were alive and conscious, but safely tied up. Lucky began to question them roughly. As he suspected, it was the vicious and ambitious Genovese who had ordered the hit. In disgust, the near-victim ordered his men to escort the assailants to the nearest airport and ensure they caught the next plane back to the States. The Mob boss also insisted they pass along a message to their employer: though Lucky might be semi-retired, he was still no pushover. If Genovese wanted to start a war, he snarled at them, he would soon know "what it feels like to have an atom bomb dropped on him."

The threat seemed to work. There were no more attempts on his life. Rather than acting as a deterrent, the incident seemed to energize the Mob boss. Lucky was more determined than ever to cling to the top spot. He was toying with the idea of retaliating with a hit on the man he ironically referred to as "Don Vitone" when he was dealt another blow. This time, word trickled back to him that there had been a fourth underworld conference — and he had not been invited.

In November 1957, Vito Genovese summoned the top names in crime to a meeting at a rural New York estate. Not everyone with an invite attended. Besides Lucky, who had not been asked to attend, two other major figures stayed well away. Frank Costello, still wrapped in bandages after the attempted assassination, wisely kept his distance. And Meyer Lansky claimed to be sick in bed with a sore throat. The so-called Apalachin Conference was meant to cement Genovese's leadership in Lucky's absence; the attendees were told to bring tribute envelopes to seal their loyalty to him.

What was meant to be Genovese's moment of triumph turned out to be a fiasco. His plan began to unravel when the sight of dozens of expensive black limousines crawling along the rural routes terrified the locals, causing the sheriff's department to investigate. A cluster of uniformed officers suddenly appeared at the doors to the mansion where the convention was being held, sending the conference-goers into a panic. The gangsters scattered like ants, leaping through windows and fleeing into the woods. Of the hundred or so attendees, 60 were captured and arrested (though just as quickly released, as there was no evidence of wrongdoing). Among them, his face bright red with shame, was the ringleader, Genovese.

Lucky Luciano was seated at his favorite restaurant, dining on a meal of spaghetti smothered with butter and cheese, when news of the raid was whispered in his ear. The Mafia leader put down his fork and mulled over the incident. Not only had Genovese attempted to stage a coup, he mused, but his foolhardy actions had very nearly destroyed the outfit Lucky had worked so hard to build. Lucky thoughtfully dabbed at his lips with a napkin. Then he excused himself, slipped into the washroom, and vomited his expensive meal into the toilet.

When he recovered from the shock, Lucky was a very angry man. Genovese was not only reckless, but "stupid," he raged, a man so blinded by ambition he had nearly wiped out the organization he had meant to take over. Lucky was disgusted that his one-time ally had forgotten his admonitions to keep a low profile. The convoy of limos was a "parade" for the locals to gawk at, he complained. "The last thing you wanna do," he said in exasperation, "is call attention to yourself."

For years, Lucky had felt his leadership slipping from his grasp. But, as he reminded himself, for now he was still boss of bosses. Since the Apalachin incident had destroyed Genovese's credibility, now was the time for Lucky to eradicate his enemy's power altogether.

Lucky's Last Stand

With the help of Lansky, Costello, and a third man, the self-effacing but wily Carlo Gambino, Lucky conspired to bring his foe to his knees. Together, they arranged to have Genovese personally handle a major drug deal, one so lucrative he would be unable to resist it. Just as the exchange was taking place, federal agents, tipped off in advance by Lucky and company, would swoop in and catch the would-be crime lord red-handed with hundreds of thousands of dollars' worth of narcotics in his possession. The police, they theorized, would burst in on the scene, guns drawn. If Genovese happened to get shot in the process, none of them would shed a tear.

It was a plan so simple it had to work, Lucky chortled to himself. But perhaps the Mob boss was getting rusty in his old age. Someone had neglected to inform the narcotics squad exactly when the deal was to occur. As a result, authorities showed up long after the transaction had taken place. Genovese walked away gleefully counting the loot, oblivious to the fact that he had been set up. The plan was an utter failure.

The second plot was a much less risky affair. The conspirators simply bribed an inmate at Sing Sing prison, Nelson Cantellops, to implicate Genovese and 24 of his top men in a drug operation. As Lucky and the others had anticipated, lawmen were so delighted to have a major criminal in their hands that they overlooked the dubious nature of the accusations. To Lucky's intense satisfaction, Vito Genovese was tried and pronounced guilty of the trumped-up charge. He would spend the rest of his life behind bars.

Lucky had triumphed over one foe, but another enemy would soon surface in his life, and this one was unconquerable, even by the boss of bosses. One day, his long-time girlfriend Igea came to him complaining of weakness and pains in her chest. Lucky was stricken to learn that his beloved had breast cancer and would require immediate surgery.

As Igea lay recuperating in her hospital bed, dozens of

floral arrangements arrived at the home they shared. They were sent by strangers from all over Italy who had read in the papers that the famous gangster's "wife" had fallen ill. In their scent-filled apartment, Lucky arranged for a prayer meeting to ask for God's intervention in Igea's illness. But it was too late. The cancer had spread throughout her body. On September 27, 1958, she murmured the words "Caro mio" in her lover's ear and quietly passed away.

Lucky's period of mourning didn't last long. By January of the next year, he had a pretty 23-year-old brunette installed in Igea's place. He had wooed Adriana Rizzo, his new girlfriend, with smooth talk and a pinch to the behind — "with Italian girls, it's a kind of compliment," he explained.

It was a surprisingly upbeat time for the faltering crime lord. He had crushed the threat from Genovese, shown he was still an effective leader in a time of crisis, and even briefly reconciled with his old friend Lansky for that one last caper. The Italian government had publicly (and mistakenly) declared him a reformed man, an "honest businessman" who deserved the same rights as any other citizen of Italy. Lucky's passport, confiscated years before, was returned to him, and the curfews and restrictions on his movements were lifted. He was still, however, forbidden to return to the U.S., even though he made a formal plea to President Eisenhower to have his exile revoked.

But Lucky's spirit of optimism didn't last. Within a month of moving in with his youthful new girlfriend, Lucky suffered his first heart attack. Though he recovered soon enough, the incident frightened him. Like Frank Costello before him, he announced his decision to retire, with pension. "Just tell 'em to send me my dough and leave me alone," he grumbled. He moved from the city to a farmhouse he had bought as an investment some years before and settled down to enjoy the simple life.

Despite Lucky's request to be left alone, the questions and demands for advice were as relentless as ever. Worse, though the couriers kept coming, the envelopes were getting lighter and lighter. Igea's illness had hit Lucky hard financially, and Castro's revolution in Cuba put an abrupt end to any profits he might reap from his investment in the Hotel Nacional. If Lansky failed to cough up a lump sum worthy of a retiring *capo*, Lucky decided, then he would look elsewhere for a big payout.

For many years, Lucky had toyed with the idea of writing his life story. "Someday," he had confided to a journalist, "I'm gonna write my own memories. Then the real story is gonna come out." In October of 1959, he made good on his threat. In a secret meeting on the resort island of Capri, he signed a contract with a movie producer. In exchange for a lump sum of $100,000 and 10 percent of the profits, he agreed, with the cautious approval of the outfit, to tell the story of his life. Though Lucky pushed the handsome, debonair actor Cary Grant as his choice to play him in the movie, the producers were leaning towards the craggy-faced, Italian-American entertainer Dean Martin for the lead role.

But back at the farm, as the Mob boss gleefully looked forward to the fame and fortune the movie would bring him, he received more bad news. His mobster cohorts back home had gotten cold feet. They realized the movie would provoke a lot of unnecessary publicity at a time when they were still attempting to regroup following the troubles and infighting of the last few years. Lucky could, if he chose, still go ahead with the project. But if he did, he was warned, he "wouldn't even be around to enjoy the profits."

The threat was effective. With the film project on hold indefinitely, Lucky flailed around, looking for revenge. His first instinct was to emerge from retirement, return to New York, and reclaim his position of power once more. Towards this end, he devised an ambitious plan. He plotted to take over the European drug trafficking industry to gain control of an area that was becoming an increasingly pivotal part of the Mafia empire. But the plan never got beyond the idea stage. It was too huge an undertaking for the ailing gangster. With little money and few allies, he realized his plan was doomed to failure. Lucky decided to start small instead. He opted to invest his time and money in a casino in Portugal and tackle more ambitious projects when the time was right.

But unbeknownst to Lucky, his renewed activity had once again attracted the attention of the police. Officials were once again tailing him and tapping his phone line. When a call came through from the movie producers telling him a "revised script" was being sent out to him, the "script" was misinterpreted as code for a drug shipment. The authorities were quick to respond. Within days, police made a fruitless raid on his home at one in the morning, sending his girlfriend into a fit of hysterics and putting undue strain on Lucky's already weakened heart.

By January 1962, the former crime boss had made definite plans to resume the film project. "I need dough bad," was his simple explanation. On the 26th of that month, in defiance of Lansky and the others, he arranged to meet with one of the producers of the proposed film biography. Accompanied by another man (allegedly an undercover narcotics agent), Lucky drove out to the Naples airport to finalize the agreement.

Moments after exiting his car, Lucky staggered, clutched at his chest, and collapsed onto unforgiving concrete. Despite the conflict of the last few months, it wasn't a Mob assassin's bullet that brought him down in the end. Perhaps it was the excitement at the thought of his comeback. Perhaps the years of official harassment had taken the ultimate toll. There, in the parking lot, as planes roared high above him, Lucky Luciano suffered a final, fatal heart attack.

****

Lucky's funeral mass was an elaborate affair, as befitted a fabled Mafia lord. Eight horses decked out with feathers pulled his hearse through the streets of Naples as spectators tearfully looked on. Though plainclothes detectives moved through the mournful crowd, hoping to make a high-profile arrest, none of Lucky's celebrated brothers in crime made an appearance. Meyer Lansky, his former best friend and *consigliere,* was nowhere in sight. Of all the old-timers, only his estranged compatriot, Joe Adonis, made a gesture of respect. He sent a wreath to his one-time bootlegging partner ornamented by a banner reading "So Long, Pal."

The only immediate member of the Luciano family to attend was the executor of Lucky's will, his younger brother Bart. He was there to sell Lucky's effects, pay off the weeping Adriana, and arrange for his brother to make his final voyage to the United States. It was on U.S. soil that Salvatore Lucania, aka Lucky Luciano, was finally buried, in a regal vault in St. John's Cathedral churchyard, in the place he had always called home: New York City.

Epilogue
The Rise of the New Bosses

The American Mafia did not die with the death of Lucky Luciano — far from it. Though the players changed, the game remained intact. New names emerged, criminals even more ruthless and vicious than those who came before. In the 1960s, there rose the almost comically ferocious Crazy Joe Gallo Gang, which kept a half-starved lion in a basement hideaway as a means of terrifying their victims into doing their bidding. Lucky's outfit, with its emphasis on obeying the rules and maintaining a low profile, seemed almost quaint and old-fashioned in contrast.

But, as Lucky once said, it was brains, not brawn alone, that got a man to the top. Waiting in the wings after the death of his leader was the ever-loyal Carlo Gambino, one of the conspirators in the downfall of Vito Genovese and a minor operator in Lucky's time. The mild-mannered Gambino had stood aside while Genovese and Anastasia self-destructed, then easily plucked their holdings to fashion his own empire. Though he died in 1976, the crime family he co-opted bears his name to this day. Its lineage can thus be traced back over 80 years, to the time of Giuseppe "Joe the Boss" Masseria. And the great, unsung mind behind the American Mafia, Meyer Lansky, died in 1983, leaving behind a net worth of an estimated $400 million.

There were many other Mafiosi who lived flashier lives and died more spectacular deaths than Lucky Luciano. Al Capone, in particular, was always more fascinating to the public than his one-time partner in crime. But when *Time* magazine published its list of the 100 most influential people of the last century, Capone's name was conspicuously absent. There, listed alongside Bill Gates and Henry Ford, was Lucky Luciano, celebrated for being the man who "organized organized crime." Lucky dragged the American Mafia from the blood feuds and arcane rituals of its Sicilian roots into the modern world. And for that, he will always be remembered.

Further Reading

Feder, Sid and Joachim Joesten. *The Luciano Story.* New York: Da Capo Press, 1954, 1994.

Gosch, Martin A. and Richard Hammer. *The Last Testament of Lucky Luciano.* Boston/Toronto: Little, Brown and Company, 1974.

Sifakis, Carl. *The Mafia Encyclopedia.* New York: Checkmark Books, 1999.

Murder, Inc.: The Story of The Syndicate. New York: Da Capo Press, 1951, 1979.

Acknowledgments

The author acknowledges the following sources for the quotes contained in the book: *The Last Testament of Lucky Luciano, The Luciano Story, The Mafia Encyclopedia,* and Time.com.

Short biographies on the major players in Luciano's life were consulted on www.crimelibrary.com.

Time.com was consulted for the magazine's article on the 100 most influential people of the century.

About the Author

Cat Klerks has a degree in English from McGill University. She is the author of *Emily Carr: The Incredible Life and Adventures of a West Coast Artist* and *The Incredible Adventures of Louis Riel: Canada's Most Famous Revolutionary,* also from Altitude Publishing. She lives and works in Banff, Alberta.